THE AMERICAN
PREJUDICE AGAINST COLOR

The American Prejudice against Color

• William G. Allen • Mary King •
• Louisa May Alcott •

Edited with an Introduction by

SARAH ELBERT

Northeastern University Press

Boston

NORTHEASTERN UNIVERSITY PRESS

LIBRARY OF CONGRESS CATALOGING-IN-PUBLICATION DATA

The American prejudice against color : William G. Allen, Mary King, and Louisa May Alcott / edited with an introduction by Sarah Elbert.

    p. cm.

    ISBN 1–55553–545–3 (pbk : alk. paper) — ISBN 1–55553–546–1 (cloth : alk. paper)

    1. Interracial marriage—United States—History—Sources. 2. Allen, William G., fl. 1849–1853. 3. Interracial marriage in literature. I. Elbert, Sarah.

    HO1031 A.494 2002

    306.84'6—dc21   2002004919

Book design and typography by Christopher Kuntze.
Composed in Monotype Plantin from Adobe Systems.
Printed and bound by The Maple Press Company in York, Pennsylvania.
The paper is Sebago Antique, an acid-free sheet.

MANUFACTURED IN THE UNITED STATES OF AMERICA

06 05 04 03 02   5 4 3 2 1

CONTENTS

INTRODUCTION

No single event more deeply stirred black and white antislavery activists in the United States and the British Isles than the passage of the American Fugitive Slave Law in 1850. Northern citizens in particular were outraged by the new federal requirement that they aid in the return of escaped slaves to their southern masters or face fines and imprisonment. The question of who was a fugitive slave and who was a "legally" free person of color was left to bounty hunters and commissioners appointed to decide each case. The commissioners received ten dollars for each human being remanded to slavery and five dollars for each soul declared free. Harriet Beecher Stowe's *Uncle Tom's Cabin* (published first as a serial in the *National Era* in 1851 and then as a two-volume novel in 1852) was the most famous literary reaction to the law, and its public impact as both a literary and a political text cannot be overestimated. Fugitive slaves found their way to Britain for twenty years prior to 1850, and they were powerful advocates in an Atlantic Abolitionist Movement, being seasoned veterans ready to resist the American Fugitive Slave Law.

In the United States, in 1852, a young quadroon scholar and abolitionist reformer, William G. Allen, wrote an enthusiastic review of *Uncle Tom's Cabin* for the *Frederick Douglass' Paper*. He found the novel thrilling: "its descriptions stir the blood" and "indeed almost make it leap out of the heart." And Allen understood and appreciated the power of Cassy, a courageous woman whose resistance overleaps the boundaries of female moral persuasion; she dares to plot vengeance and murder for the fate of her daughters and the abuse she has suffered. Allen wrote of Cassy that her story was more than "anything I have ever read, in all that is soul searching and thrilling." (Allen was in his second year as professor of the "Greek and German languages, and of Rhetoric and Belles-Lettres of New York Central College, situated in McGrawville, Cortland Country,—the only College in America that has ever called a colored man to a Professorship, and one of the very few that receive colored and white students on terms of perfect equality, if, indeed, they receive colored students at all.")

Allen rejected Stowe's colonization solution for the fictional quadroon couple, George and Eliza, and argued instead that George Harris was quite right to reject bondage but not right to desire instead "an African nationality." Allen insisted on first-class citizenship in the country of his own birth. He would not accept colonization in Liberia as a solution to his own oppression, nor would he accept colonization as African Americans' mission to civilize Africa. Stowe's hero, George Harris, said he would "cast in my lot" with the "oppressed enslaved African race." Allen proudly claimed the heritage of his own mulatta mother, but he also insisted that "the talk about African nationality . . . is sheer nonsense." Historian Tavia Nyong'o recently uncovered the layered meanings in Allen's letters to the *Frederick Douglass' Paper*. Thanks to this sensitive, historicized reading of the racial and sexual debates, we can see Allen in his narratives working toward an even more cogent defense of "amalgamation," or social integration of the races in America. In the letters to Douglass's paper, Allen presented a spiritual universalism in which "nations, there must be, but merely as conveniences, not to abrogate the great law of equal brotherhood." It was his further belief that, in terms of the cultural and social evolution of human beings, "nations worthy of the name, are only produced by a fusion of races."

In other words, to William G. Allen amalgamation was natural because all humans are the children of God, made in his image; to think that one group of human beings is better or "higher" than another is, as Nyong'o correctly reads Allen, a "sinful prejudice." At the same time there remains an unresolved intellectual contradiction in Allen's speeches and writings that was present in the many serious debates about race and nationality and sex in the mid-nineteenth century. Abolitionists' and anti-abolitionists' debates often seemed confused and contradictory, arguing either that all races were one race in God's creation or that each race had developed unequally or perhaps

2

even been created separately. "Nation," "race," and "the human race" were all used interchangeably, with the result that our confusion mirrors that of mid-nineteenth-century culture and society. Some argued that each nation or race had specific traits or gifts that must be kept intact through what the Spanish called "limpieza de sangre," purity of the blood. Since the "white" race (Europeans, for the most part) had the most advanced civilization, legal marriages between white men and women had to be protected in order to preserve that superiority. This racial superiority "naturally" brought with it what historian David Roediger has called "the wages of whiteness": presumed racial purity and superiority merited land, political power, preference in hiring and admittance to schools, and more. Reproducing their racial and class privileges was a serious concern of gentlemen of property and standing. Making sure that their lesser but still important "wages of whiteness" were secured concerned the white working class mobs who protested any form of "amalgamation," including integrated schooling and intermarriage. Being "white" could even trump class differences in politics and culture.

Some reformers argued that individuals and society at large were enhanced through "amalgamation" in all its forms. They were sure that freedom of association between men and women, blacks and whites, rich and poor fostered universal improvement of the human race. Free and open social association better controlled Passion, which was dangerous when it led to unbridled physicality and instinctual behavior. Secrets only made the presumed differences between the sexes and races all the more dangerously alluring. Positions on race were often—though not always—parallel to positions on the sexes; conservatives insisted that sexual differences included intellectual and emotional gifts as well as biological givens. Further, sexual differences, along with a sexual division of labor, must be preserved to guarantee a balanced, symmetrical society. Women entering the public sphere of male commerce and politics would quickly coarsen their tender sensibilities and become just like men. There would thence be no refuge for anyone from the cruel and heartless world of the marketplace and no domestic haven in which women (like Mrs. Senator Bird in *Uncle Tom's Cabin*) could gently persuade men to "feel right" and do right by their fellow human beings, slave or free.

The proponents of woman's rights, on the other hand, argued that differences between men and women had reached such an unnatural state as to produce dangerously "separate spheres." Society needed woman to extend her sphere outward to create one great human family. The most radical abolitionists and woman's rights advocates favored full social amalgamation to create an integrated society of individuals perfected in female kindness, spirituality, and self-sacrifice in concert with male rationality, courage, and enterprise. These "amalgamated" bodies associated freely and formed institutions ranging from coeducational, integrated schools to marriages, same-sex friendships across racial lines, free churches, intentional communities, and, finally, new political parties. In the antebellum period any mixed-race public assembly, especially one with both men and women present, was denounced as a "promiscuous assembly." Abolitionist meetings were attacked by mobs, and the press reported promiscuous gatherings and amalgamation with savage derision. Schools that dared both coeducation and racial integration risked public censure at the very least and mob violence at the worst.

In 1853 William G. Allen was rather well known in the "North Star" abolitionist community as the "Colored Professor" of New York Central College, a few miles from Syracuse. Professor Allen was not a fugitive slave when he fled to England that year. Nevertheless, he and his white bride, Mary King Allen, were indeed fugitives, fleeing for their lives from "the American Prejudice Against Color," as he called his narrative of their ordeal. They met and fell in love at the college, where Mary King was a local student, the daughter of a Methodist minister in Fulton, New York, a small village near Syracuse. Her father and one of her brothers were active abolitionists, and William Allen was invited to their home when he lectured in Fulton. Mary King's family sanctioned their early friendship. Over a year later, after a discreet courtship, the couple was seriously considering marriage with, it then seemed, her family's acceptance. In his Narrative we read, 150 years later, Allen's crisp, ironic voice recounting the event that changed their lives: "The mob occurred on Sabbath (!) evening, January the 30th, 1853, in the village of Phillipsville, near Fulton, Oswego County, New York. The cause,—the intention, on my part, of marrying a white young lady of Fulton,—at least so the public surmised."

Allen's account was published in Dublin, Edinburgh, and London. Since Allen is a refugee, readers perfectly understand that there are many more such witnesses of systemic barbarism. Moreover, the Preface gives detailed extracts from a number of well-known British and American abolitionists who introduce Allen to what we may assume is an already sympathetic and knowledgeable audience. George Thompson, in particular, mentions that Allen is a free person of color and recommends not only Allen himself to the reader, but "still more your heroic and most estimable lady." The reasons that Mary King Allen justly merits such praise are clearly revealed in Allen's account of his wife's steadfast devotion in the face not only of mob violence and family betrayal, but also in the face of the white public's uproar over an interracial marriage as a particularly radical expression of amalgamation.

Only a few years later, in 1860, Allen repeats much of his story, but in a more personal and desperate tone. *A Short Personal Narrative* was published in Dublin (and "sold by the author"). Allen is writing his pamphlet not only to serve the cause but also and importantly to make a bit of money to support his family; things are not going so well after seven years abroad.

A free person of color, adopted by well-to-do colored parents, Allen overcame the barriers to education and commended "kind-hearted" slaveholders who aided him. Nevertheless, he never forgot the cry of the auctioneer in Norfolk, Virginia: "What will you give for this man?" "What for this woman?" "What for this child?" Allen describes the course of his education and his rise in enterprise in the northern "free" states, and

5

his good fellowship with abolitionists both white and black. He becomes accustomed to open, free associations built on the recognizable merit of his character and accomplishments. He then returns to Virginia hoping to see his childhood home and friends again. Allen is met with the scorn of Norfolk whites and their threat of enslavement or worse now that his connections with Oneida Institute, an "abolition college," are known. Unquestionably, even before his courtship and marriage William Allen knew that he could not go home again. He was an outcast in both the North and South of the United States, and part of Mary King Allen's heroism lies in her joining her life and fortunes to him beside an outcast fire.

My own first reading of his pamphlets was in the Samuel J. May Anti-Slavery Collection at Cornell University, a gift of the Reverend May, a Unitarian minister in Syracuse, and, incidentally, the brother of Abigail May Alcott and the favorite uncle of Louisa May Alcott, who visited her uncle and his family in Syracuse during the year of Willam Allen and Mary King's ordeal. These two carefully bound pamphlets are inscribed to Samuel J. May.

Several questions arose as I read these narratives. Within these pages William G. Allen never details his own impressive history as an abolitionist organizer, activist, and scholar. Does he presume that his readers already know his accomplishments? Or is Allen strategically presenting himself as a quadroon gentleman who is innocent of political agitation and guilty only of acquiring a distinguished education and developing a dignified friendship with an educated white woman, a friendship that slowly becomes true love and is then sanctified by marriage? Allen does not explain the meanings of the events and terms he graphically describes in the narratives. He does not tell readers what a "Mary Rescue" or a "Fulton Rescue" is (he refers to the famous "Jerry Rescue"—about which more later—which preceded Allen's trials in Syracuse). And why does he not explain what the Fugitive Slave Law meant for African Americans born enslaved or free who had to flee through western New York to Canada after 1850? Allen himself was active in aiding and educating fugitives in both New York and Canada. He does mention his study of law with Ellis Loring in Boston, but not a word appears about Loring's impressive abolitionist politics and practice, which surely informed Allen's legal education.

Finally, we are faced with the long-term exile of the Allen family in the United Kingdom. They did not, so far as we know, ever return to the United States, even after the Civil War. We must then fill in, as best we can, some details of their lives and the North Star abolitionist network, in which were powerful friendships that sustained the couple in their courtship, marriage, and exile. Some possible answers to their continued residence abroad may suggest themselves if we briefly consider trans-Atlantic abolitionists' battles with "the American prejudice against color" throughout the period.

The North Star Network

A few miles from Phillipsville, Samuel Joseph May's congregation in Syracuse admired both his moral courage and his tender sensibilities. He was engaged in perfecting "the abolitionist church," where universal fellowship aimed to erase all distinctions "of race, wealth, social position, culture . . . or sectarian belief." Samuel May was a friend and ally to organized black abolitionists in western New York. His modern biographer, Donald Yacovone, reconstructs May's vision of race and gender reformation from his 1850 writings: "A perfect character in either man or woman is a compound of the virtues and graces of each. The Excellencies which each sex most needs are objective to it in the other sex. In Jesus . . . we see as much feminine as masculine grace."

Allen's *Short Personal Narrative* and his autobiographical antislavery pamphlet, *The American Prejudice Against Color,* remained safely but obscurely in archival boxes among May's personal papers and pamphlet collection in Cornell University's Anti-Slavery Collection. Allen has remained "the Forgotten Professor," as the historian R. J. M. Blackett writes. May is the subject of many laudatory texts and his Syracuse church is now called the May Memorial Church. May gave his papers and pamphlets to Cornell's President Andrew Dickson White, in support of White's promise to welcome students of all races and both sexes. Nevertheless, it took almost one hundred years— and the post–World War II G.I. Bill, and then the 1960s Civil Rights Movement—to accelerate substantial national college admissions of men and women of all races and classes. And these graduates in turn forged the women's history, African American history, and multicultural history and literary criticism that challenged canons, theories, and analyses and produced documentary editions, archival projects, and revisionist texts. Our understanding of William G. and Mary King Allen's lives and work is made possible through studying *The Black Abolitionist Papers*, edited by Peter C. Ripley; Harriet Wilson's *Our Nig;* Louisa May Alcott's abolitionist tales; Milton Sernett's inspiring books, two of which are *Abolition's Axe: Beriah Green, Oneida Institute, and the Black Freedom Struggle* and *North Star Country: Upstate New York and the Crusade for African American Freedom*; reprints of William Allen's pamphlets; and R. J. M. Blackett's thoroughly researched 1980 account, "William J. Allen, the Forgotten Professor," in *Civil War History*.

Perhaps the persistent naturalization of social categories and the policing of boundaries can explain why there was, seemingly, no popular knowledge of the history of African Americans, which, as Blackett writes, is "littered with a depressing number of important but forgotten individuals, men and women who resisted oppression and fought for a new world free from racial inequalities." There was fiction by writers both black and white on this struggle, but generally male and female writers followed one of several conventional alternatives for ending a story with a biracial hero: escape and then emigration; death and salvation through a white soul in a black body; or emancipation mandated by enlightenment "natural rights" and brought about by a true woman's efforts. For example, William Wells Brown, an African American writer, offered an important model in *Clotel: or, The President's Daughter* (1853); his hero is a "white slave" and, like George and Eliza Harris in *Uncle Tom's Cabin*, he

8

rebels, escapes, and "passes" into freedom with the help of a true woman.

The courtship of William G. Allen and Mary King occupies merely fifteen pages of his hundred-page *Authentic Narrative*. The rest, as we say, "is history," which usually means that it is over and forgotten, as Blackett reminds us. Samuel J. May's diaries for the period were unfortunately lost in May's house fire, but they are not the only records of the North Star abolitionists and the interracial friendships and true loves forged in active amalgamation. William G. Allen's character endorsements give us markers with which to trace these relationships and close the historical gaps. Gerrit Smith, the upstate New York philanthropist and radical abolitionist, is included, along with two British notables, Joseph Sturge and George Thompson, for their efforts to introduce Allen and find opportunities for him to give lectures on abolition and "American topics, including the social position of the free colored population." All three white abolitionists were well known to both the Mays and the Alcotts; Abigail May Alcott, Samuel May's sister and Louisa's mother, hid George Thompson's portrait when an anti-abolitionist mob threatened his life. Thompson received letters from Samuel May and Gerrit Smith in support of the Allens. Allen had fond memories of his education at Oneida Institute in Whitesboro, New York, from which he graduated in 1844. Oneida was headed by Beriah Green. Besides working for their tuition and subsistence and mastering a full classical curriculum there, many students, like Allen, were active abolitionists; several of Allen's fellow alumni became leaders in the North Star movement: Henry Highland Garnet, Samuel Ringgold Ward, and Jermain W. Loguen.

Sernett traces the history of the Oneida Institute, New York Central College, and the abolitionist generation who called upstate New York "North Star country"—after the masthead of Frederick Douglass's famous newspaper, *North Star,* and the polar star that guided fugitives from slavery to freedom. In *North Star Country* Sernett describes Oneida Institute of Science and Industry, located in a converted farmhouse along the Erie

Canal, near Utica in the village of Whitesboro. It opened in 1827 with a contingent of Charles Finney's evangelical converts, who found their new school organized on the Swiss model for poor young people. Their manual labor and education were combined to foster healthy minds and healthy bodies. Within a few years Oneida was a thriving establishment: students milked cows, worked in the fields, and studied a classical curriculum.

William Lloyd Garrison's call for immediate abolition of slavery was enthusiastically received at Oneida, though not by everyone; rival antislavery factions joined in active debate. Beriah Green, a devoted Garrisonian, an opponent of colonization, and a professor at Western Reserve College, was invited by the trustees to lead Oneida Institute. He arrived in 1833 with the understanding that the school would be open to black and white students alike. What followed can well be called a barnstorming abolitionist campaign. In the next year the Whitestone Abolitionist Society was formed, as was the Smithfield Society, in Gerrit Smith's hometown of Peterboro, and another society was organized in Utica. Beriah Green won over Theodore Dwight Weld, perhaps after Garrison the most well known white abolitionist, to the cause of immediate abolition. After mobs in New York City and Utica destroyed abolitionists' property and attacked free black citizens, Gerrit Smith (who was a cousin of Elizabeth Cady Stanton), perhaps the wealthiest landowner in western New York, was converted as well. His generous contributions to the cause included his support of Oneida Institute and then the founding of New York Central College at McGrawville. The intensity and courage of these activists are all the more remarkable because they acted before the establishment of any national society for immediate abolition. Finally, in December 1833 a national convention was held in Philadelphia; Beriah Green was chosen as president. Among the women present was Lucretia Mott, the Quaker abolitionist and woman's rights advocate. Green invited her to speak, saying, "Go on ma'am, go on; we shall be glad to hear you." Samuel May was there, a young Boston clergyman, newly graduated and ordained from Harvard's Unitarian Divinity School. May remarked that Green "proved to be a man in whom there was 'timber' enough to make half a dozen Presidents, if the Convention had needed so many."

In Gerrit Smith's papers at Syracuse University, there is a letter from Beriah Green, testifying to William G. Allen's potential. Dated December 10, 1840, Green introduces Mr. Allen as a "young man of high promise." He was setting out that day for Peterboro, New York, and while talented, he was "very poor" and "very poorly clad." Green hoped that some of Smith's neighbors "might find a pleasure in assisting so deserving a youth in this particular. He has made great progress in his studies, his conduct is remarkably good." Green added, "I hope you will hear him on his flute. He used to assist the choir in the chapel with it. I have heard him highly spoken of for his skill by such as I know to be good judges." He faithfully attended church, but Green could not speak confidently yet about the "the state of his heart—Christ-wise."

The state of Allen's intellect and his knowledge of politics and law a few years later is more certain; he himself tells us that, having graduated "with some honors" from Oneida, he studied law with Ellis Gray Loring in Boston; Blackett dates the clerkship in Loring's office as beginning in 1847. In Boston for several volatile years, Allen was active in the abolitionist community, giving lectures entitled "History, Literature, and the Destiny of the African Race." He wrote the introduction for an edition of essays on Phillis Wheatley, Benjamin Banneker, and James Moses Horton, to familiarize his audience with "the contributions of the African Race to civilization." Phillis Wheatley's elegant poetry had astonished white readers in colonial America; Benjamin Banneker wrote to Thomas Jefferson in 1791, "freely and cheerfully" acknowledging that he was "of the African Race" and insisting on appreciation of Africa's great heritage; James Moses Horton, an enslaved North Carolina poet, wrote "In Hope of Liberty," and his poems led Northern black abolitionists to try, if unsuccessfully, to emancipate Horton.

Allen, along with Samuel Ringgold Ward, Henry Highland Garnet, Samuel May, and Louisa May Alcott, advocated amal-

gamation to strengthen the new American race. Allen wrote in
Frederick Douglass's paper, "The greatness of the American
nation is unquestionably owing no less to the various elements
of which it is composed, than to its climate and favorable circumstances." Allen publicly engaged with the free black and
white abolitionist community in demands for complete social
equality. His doing so would have been no impediment to his
work for Ellis Loring. Loring, a close friend of Samuel J. May
and an occasional legal advisor to May's family, was also a friend
and former schoolmate of Ralph Waldo Emerson. Along with
Garrison and May, Loring was one of the first organizers of the
New England Anti-Slavery Society. His marriage to Louisa
Gilman provided a home for antislavery workers of all colors as
well as for fugitive slaves. Legal history records his argument for
the slave Med, brought to Massachusetts by her mistress; on
habeas corpus proceedings Loring won the case for her, estab-
lishing the principle that a slave brought voluntarily into
Massachusetts could not be removed from the state against his
or her will. Loring's financial support of *The Liberator* saved that
abolitionist paper from closing several times.

William Allen does not, in these narratives, refer to his activ-
ities in Boston or to his personal relationship with Loring or to
the lawyer's famous abolitionism. He says nothing of his own
well thought-out, researched, and publicly argued position on
amalgamation and progress. But we have a report in the
Liberator of August 30, 1850, citing the Cazenovia, New York,
Convention of two thousand participants, with Frederick
Douglass presiding and singing by the Elmore sisters, which
Allen may have attended. *The Liberator* quotes from the *Essex
County Freeman* on a "very able and interesting lecture delivered
last Tuesday Evening in the vestry of the Old South Church in
Danvers, by Mr. William G. Allen, a colored law student of
Boston, on the 'Origin and History of the Africans.'" It is worth
reproducing here in full:

Mr. Allen commenced with the somewhat startling assertion, that
the Africans originated the arts and sciences, and gave the first
impulse to civilization. How different this idea from the notion

entertained by great numbers in this country, at the present day, some of whom would endeavor to persuade themselves and others to believe that the Negro is but a mere connecting link between the brute creation and the human race! But the speaker sustained his position by the most irrefutable proofs, drawn from the past history of the world, evincing a depth of research to which few men of any profession can lay claim. He seemed indeed to be perfectly familiar with every branch of the human family, as far back as the days of Noah, and to possess an intimate acquaintance with all the writings extant of every historian, both ancient and modern.

With one stroke of his logic, he let the wind out of that sophistical argument put forth the last year in a pamphlet entitled "Thoughts on Slavery," in which the author endeavors to prove, by the curse pronounced upon Canaan, that Southern slavery is a Bible institution sanctioned by the God of heaven!

Proceeding in this lecture, Mr. A. runs a tilt against Prof. Agassiz, who has recently made an attack upon Divine Revelation, by denying that "God made of one blood all nations of men to dwell on all the face of the earth," and completely unhorsing him, knocked him back into the dark ages to flounder on through the chaos of his own conflicting opinions with Linnaeus, Buffon, Helvetius, Monboddo and Darwin—men who once advocated the same absurd theory, that the human race originated from different sources.

Mr. A. also showed that the diversities among the different nations of mankind were produced by the influence which climate, hard treatment and different kinds of food had upon the animal frame and the color of the skin.

The lecture was one, which would have done honor to the mind of the historian Bancroft, while the gentle and modest demeanor of the speaker, together with the gracefulness of his elocution and ready command of language, gave the performance an additional interest.

We understand that at the close of the meeting, one or two profound eurodites left the vestry complaining that the lecturer had not given the true origins of the blacks which they said was Cain, upon whom the Almighty placed a mark for the crime of murdering his brother and from whom the negroes sprung.

We should hardly know how to get along with this theory of the origins of true Africans, unless we suppose that some one of Cain's descendents (all of whom it is generally thought were swept away by the deluge) plunged to the bottom of the mighty flood which then mantled the entire globe as with a garment, and secreting himself in some subterranean cavern to keep from being dashed against the rocks or devoured by a sea-monster, held his breath till the waters had subsided, when he came out from his hiding-place, walked abroad in the earth, married one of old Noah's grand-daughters and commenced again peopling the world with a race of negroes.

This issue of *The Liberator* carried a note of national impor-tance, "Still Debating Fugitive Slave Bill," followed by an announcement of a "Woman's Convention to be held October 23, 24 [1850]," with the signatures of the Garrisons, Lucy Stone, Wendell Phillips, Paulina Wright Davis, Charlotte May (a cousin of Samuel J. May), Lucretia Mott, and others.

Allen tells his readers that after Boston he was called to a pro-fessorship at New York Central College. The college had opened in 1849, after Oneida Institute closed; it was sponsored by the American Baptist Free Mission Society. The new college presi-dent was Elder C. P. Grovesnor who championed women's right to an education equal to men's; by definition, he felt, separate was not equal. Gerrit Smith, Frederick Douglass, William Lloyd Garrison, Samuel Ringgold Ward, and Horace Greeley all made financial contributions. The college had an imposing four-story brick building, which housed a preparatory school and the col-lege; there were also several farm outbuildings and land to be worked. Women made up about one-third of the student body, which included the famous Edmundson sisters, who had escaped slavery in Washington, D.C., and Edmonia Lewis, the sculptor whose heritage included both native Americans and African Americans. As had been true at Oneida, manual work and a classical curriculum went hand in hand. As a coeduca-tional, amalgamated college, following Frederick Douglass's principle, "All Rights for All," New York Central College was denied financial support by the New York State Legislature and it was bankrupt by 1858; it closed forever in 1861.

In the spring of 1851 Allen says he was invited to speak in Fulton, a few miles from McGrawville and about twenty-five miles from Syracuse. In Fulton he delivered a series of lectures and spent several days there at the home of the Reverend Lyndon King, a "devoted" abolitionist and advocate of the social, political, and religious rights of "the colored man." He met the Reverend King's daughter Mary in her home; she was about to enter the college in McGrawville. A college student for a year and half, she lived in a boardinghouse across the street from Allen's own lodgings, and they "freely conversed." Allen forthrightly details their equality: she was of "full age, and legally, as well as intellectually and morally, competent to discuss the subjects in which, it is generally supposed, young men and women feel an absorbing interest." In due time teacher and pupil formed a reciprocal affection, though Allen discreetly avoids the word "love."

In September 1852 Gerrit Smith wrote to the *Pennsylvania Freeman* describing the "Central College of New York."

Samuel Aaron, Norristown
T. B. Hudson, Oberlin

My Dear Sirs, —I have just returned from my first visit to Central College. Let me tell you a few of the very pleasant things I saw there.

1st. The sexes are educated together. The nonsense, that there is a feminine element in the human mind and a masculine element in the human mind is regarded there as nonsense. About two-fifths of the students are females.

2d. A part of the teachers are females.

3d. About one-fifth of the students are colored persons.

4th. One of the professors is a colored person.

5th. No student is known to use profane language.

6th. No student is known to use intoxicating drinks.

7th. No student is known to use tobacco.

8th. Water is the only drink in the Boarding House. Not having drank tea or coffee for nearly twenty years, I felt quite at home in sitting at a table among scores of water-drinkers.

9th. Not the least pleasant thing, that I saw there, is the prospect (I say not how bright) that a Church will be speedily gathered, under the name of "The Church of McGrawville." Its distinctive principle will be, that *the Christians of the place are the church of the place:*—not *ought* to be—not *must* be—*but* ARE the church of the place. Such a full recognition of the rights of the Christian brotherhood, added to her present full recognition of the rights of the human brotherhood, will make Central College the desire of many eyes and the joy of many hearts.

10th. "Beautiful for situation is" Central College.

I am constrained to admit, that I saw one unpleasant thing in Central College. This unpleasant thing is the empty Presidential Chair—empty, because neither of you will consent to fill it.

The Post Office of Central College is McGrawville, Cortland County N. Y.

It must be noted that Gerrit Smith's combination of amalgamation, woman's rights, immediate abolition, and temperance was the product of his own powerful evangelical conversion on the event of his second marriage. He had in his youth been something of a dandy; he drank and enjoyed the ladies and his own position as the handsome, wealthy son of the largest landholder in western New York. However, after his mother's death shortly after his graduation from Hamilton College and his father's retirement, Smith was the only one of his brothers who was not an alcoholic or mentally ill. He felt a serious responsibility, which he honored. He lost his first wife through her early death. Smith grew personally and politically, and he had a distinguished political career as well as a long and happy family life. Perhaps his only personal encounter with the dangers of abolition and amalgamation arose from his support of John Brown as a member of the Secret Six. Smith risked imprisonment for his action, and he signed himself briefly into an insane asylum— possibly to avoid legal harassment.

In 1851 the North Star group near Syracuse, New York, was joined by Samuel Ringgold Ward, a fugitive from slavery and a brilliant African American orator, ordained by the New York Congregational Association. He had ministered to a white congregation in Wayne County, New York, from 1841 through 1843. He moved to Syracuse, where he published the *Impartial Citizen,* an abolitionist newspaper supported by Henry Garnet and his wife, Julia, who led a group of African American women in fund-raising efforts for the newspaper. At the Woman's Rights Convention in Rochester, New York, in 1853 Frederick Douglass joined the causes of abolition and woman's rights, not for the first time; he had a powerful ally there with Jermain Loguen, the African American preacher from Syracuse who had spearheaded the "Jerry Rescue" of 1851 and was named a vice-president of the convention.

William Allen and Mary King were part of this active group of people fighting the twin bastions of racial and sexual prejudice. In December 1852 they discussed marriage and "surveyed" all of the "difficulties, embarrassments, trials, insults and persecutions" attendant upon their "diversity of complexion." They separated to deliberate further; Allen remarked that while this might seem "unromantic" to readers, it was "prudent." Allen's tribute to Mary King and his explanation of the social consequences of her decision must be read carefully because they are at the heart of Allen's amalgamation brief as the basis of freedom and democracy.

I will not speak of myself, but on the part of Miss King, this was certainly a bold step. It displayed a moral heroism which no one can comprehend who has not been in America, and who does not understand the diabolical workings of prejudice against color. Whatever a man may be in his own person,—though he should have the eloquence, talents, and character of Paul and Apollos, and the Angel Gabriel combined,—though he should be as wealthy as Croesus,—and though, in personal appearance, he should be as fair as the fairest Anglo-Saxon, yet, if he have but one drop of the blood of the African flowing in his veins, no white lady can ally herself to him in matrimony, without bringing upon her the anathemas of the community, with scarcely an exception, and rendering herself an almost total outcast, not only from the society in which she formerly moved, but from society in general.

Allen recounts a well-known abolitionist story in which a planter was in love with a quadroon girl and, wishing to marry her, injected himself with the blood of one of his slaves in order to satisfy the law of Louisiana that her husband be a man with African blood. He goes on to caution the reader that marriage between black and white is not the custom; rather women of color are completely without protection in the slave states, and in the North no white man would "lose his caste" by debauching a colored woman, but "would be mobbed from Maine to Delaware, should he with that same woman attempt honorable marriage."

Having thus educated his British readers about American caste, Allen returns to the narrative. Miss King consulted her father before their engagement and he consented, as did her sister. Her several brothers were bitterly opposed. "Mrs. King—a step-mother only—was not only also bitterly opposed, but *inveterately* so." Here Allen's description is remarkably similar to that of the villainess in Harriet Wilson's autobiographical novel, *Our Nig: or, Sketches from the Life of a Free Black, in a Two-Story White House, North, Showing That Slavery's Shadows Fall Even There* (1859). Mrs. King had a certain benevolence, and she prided herself on pitying the fugitive and permitting him at her table. But she was "extremely aristocratic of heart and patronizing of temper." In short, she was a snob, and while she loudly professed her Christianity, her racism expressed itself in violent acts, angry torrents of speech, and jealous domination of the household. Harriet Wilson sketches the same profile of Mrs. Bellmont, the mistress who abuses Frado and dominates the household in *Our Nig.*

Mary King and Louisa May Alcott's heroine Claudia in her abolitionist-amalgamation tale, "M.L.," are as sisters in character and soul. Mary King's letter to William Allen upon their engagement seems a model for Alcott's heroine: "I have endeavored to solve, honorably, conscientiously and judiciously, the greatest problem of human life; and God and the holy angels have assisted me in thus solving. Friends may forsake me, and the world prove false, but the sweet assurance that I have your most devoted love, and that that love will strengthen and increase in proportion as the regard of others may diminish, is the only return I ask."

From here the two stories diverge dramatically; Alcott writes a happy ending that would have been sorely compromised by historical reality. Whiteness was a privilege in republican America, and a most carefully constructed and policed privilege. Poor, working-class, and middle-class citizens of European origin were united in claiming a caste distinction that guaranteed them what Alcott called "a perch on the ladder." Historians recently have researched and analyzed the "making of whiteness," or "How the Irish Became White," or "How Jews Became White Folks." In "M.L." the "social suicide" committed by amalgamation is kept within discrete though certainly painful boundaries. It is a private "family affair" to the end, perhaps kept beyond the reach of public violence by Alcott's endowing Claudia with wealth and "orphan" status. Alcott aims to soothe and inspire her readers to accept amalgamation as consonant with true love and Christian fidelity. Nevertheless, Alcott almost certainly knew of William G. Allen and Mary King. Alcott's sister Anna was living with the Mays, and Louisa Alcott visited her there. And the Allen-King story was reprinted in abolitionist newspapers regularly read by the Alcotts.

Allen, however, says, "Family opposition was not the only opposition which Miss King expected to, or did indeed encounter." The public soon learned of the engagement; some thought the marriage already accomplished, and "public opposition ... soon began to assume a more decided form." The King household was besieged with neighbors decrying the outrage, predicting Heaven's revenge upon the family and the community. Meanwhile, there were two friends of the young couple, Mr. and Mrs. Porter, schoolteachers and fellow graduates of McGrawville who lived nearby in Phillipsville, which was the railroad depot for Fulton residents. Of all the families in neighboring towns of some two thousand people, only this one couple publicly approved of the lovers' engagement. Mary King's brother John was a "reform" minister, preaching in Washington, D.C., and raising money for a church that would exclude slaveholders; but, arriving in Fulton, he furiously opposed the match. To Allen this was the grossest form of betrayal. John King averred that if Allen had "the remaining fourth Anglo-Saxon blood, he would be proud of [Allen] as a brother." As things stood, he barred Allen from any visit to the household, save as a driver or servant. For Allen this was the crisis moment: the dispute moved from private to public outrage because Mary King's father could not resist the combined opposition of her stepmother and her elder brother. Mary then had to do without her father's support as he, a declared abolitionist minister, banished Allen from the house. But, strangely enough, at the same moment on Saturday, January 29, her father drove Mary to Phillipsville to meet her fiancé, and it was this move that placed the couple in danger of their lives from the Fulton mob. Allen believed that, had the matter been kept private, within the household, "Christian propriety," reason, and experience would have resolved their differences peaceably.

It was not to be so. The next day, the couple was visiting in the Porters' Phillipsville home when a "gentleman . . . decidedly opposed to 'amalgamation'" arrived and informed the company that they *"were to be mobbed."* All Fulton had been up in arms since the previous night, crowds gathering in the streets, while "tar, feathers, poles, and an empty barrel spiked with shingle nails had been prepared" for Allen. It was, as he writes, "escape or death." Porter thought that moving Allen to a neighbor's house would foil the mob, and that the matter would then "blow quietly over." While they discussed options, however, the mob was upon them "like wild beasts out of a den." There were first twenty men turning the corner, then thirty or forty, and "soon the streets were filled with men—some four or five hundred. . . . there was driven a sleigh in which, we rightly conjectured, Miss King was to be taken home."

A committee within the mob was self-constituted, and these gentlemen acted as a delegation to Allen, King, and the Porters, while also attempting to "quiet the mob spirit." Allen minces no words about cross-class racism: "In this, more than in anything else did the malignant character of this American feeling evince itself—that to drive me off or kill me, if need be, the 'respectable' and the base were commingled, like—'kindred elements into one.' . . . They meant no more than to save the honor of their village by preventing, if possible, bloodshed and death. They were not men of better principles than the rabble—they were only men of better breeding."

The committee saved Allen's life, and his public thank-you was similar to the gratitude he would have expressed to someone "who took deadly aim . . . with his revolver, and only missed his mark." Allen was well aware that his death would have been neither swift nor easy: "Previous to the death which I was to suffer in the spiked barrel, I was to undergo various torturing and mutilations of person, aside from the tarring and feathering—some of these mutilations too shocking to be named in the pages of this book." Allen assures his readers that this incident was by no means extraordinary in a country where the life of a colored man is "less sacred than that of a dog."

The American newspapers he quotes from contain accounts of colored passengers beaten on boats and cars and colored ladies ejected from seats so that white "loafers" might be seated. These incidents also appear in the antislavery papers, which published Louisa May Alcott's abolitionist stories before and during the Civil War. Her own clippings from *Commonwealth* include the report of a widow of a soldier in the 26th U.S. Colored Troops ejected from her seat on the Eighth Avenue cars, a particularly profane act in the eyes of the abolitionist witness.

Allen says that Miss King left the village accompanied by committee members, whispering that she would meet him the next day in Syracuse. The rest of the men moved Allen to the village hotel in order to save the Porters' house from mob destruction. He passed through a gauntlet of lynch mobbers who hit him and tore at his clothing, yelling obscenities as he hurried toward the hotel, a quarter of a mile away. From there Professor Allen (and they emphasized the "Professor") was conveyed by sleigh, for which he paid six dollars, to Syracuse! The mob leader, Henry Hibbard, subsequently published his own account, "Another Rescue," in the *Syracuse Star*, which was, as Allen notes, "one of the organs of the Fillmore Administration." Hibbard's account refers to Mr. King's church as a "regular Wesleyan Methodist, Abolition, Amalgamation Church" and the college as a "nigger" institution, while Professor Allen is described as an "anti-alabaster Sambo." The semiliterate, explosive account is purposefully quoted in full; some contextualization is required for the modern reader to appreciate fully this and other local newspaper accounts he copies.

Garrison opposed political means to end slavery, favoring

nonresistance and disassociation; he famously declared, "no union with slaveholders," and "the Constitution of the United States is a 'covenant with death' and agreement with hell." Samuel J. May, like William Allen, moved from a rejection of party politics to a belief that the political system, and particularly the Liberty Party and then the Free Soil Party, and the Republican Party could be used to win abolition and black rights. Neither man, however, completely rejected the possibility of "disunionism," or the strategy of disassociating from the Union as a slave state (because the Union was itself a "slave state"), though the Alcotts, Mays, and Allen himself were antislavery Unionists, and indeed nationalists. May supported a convention to name Gerrit Smith as a presidential candidate in 1848. Nevertheless, in August of that year he joined black leaders and white abolitionists at the Buffalo convention in which "Barn Burner Democrats" and "Conscience Whigs" supported the former Democratic president Martin Van Buren of New York. Donald Yacovone concludes that May probably did so believing that Van Buren could be "controlled." He was in good company with Henry Bibb and Samuel Ringgold Ward, as well as Frederick Douglass and Henry Stanton, but the new Free Soil Party with Van Buren at its head garnered only ten percent of the popular vote.

May was prescient in his assessment of 1848 as the year signaling profound political and social changes throughout the world. Daniel Webster supported the Fugitive Slave Bill in order to preserve the Union in 1850, and Boston's "men of property and standing" publicly thanked him for his address. This was a fact surely referred to by Allen in his condemnation of the committee as men of "better breeding" but no better principles than the mob. The Fugitive Slave Law galvanized many white abolitionists, including the peace-loving Samuel May and certainly the more volatile Louisa May Alcott, from nonresistance to civil disobedience and even to support of open armed warfare (as evidenced by the family's support of John Brown). English Unitarians praised the Reverend May among others for a militant abolitionist stand. And the Fugitive Slave Law made western New York and Syracuse in particular a destination for fugitives slaves, as thousands of them headed to Canada. The Reverend May was among the most active Underground Railway conductors and fund-raisers, and an "expert on the black Canadian settlements." William G. Allen, according to Blackett, had taught in a school for fugitive slaves in Canada in the summer of 1841, and it is quite likely that Allen was involved in the efforts to send money, Bibles, and clothing to Canada. The American Anti-Slavery Society met in Syracuse in March 1851; the speakers included George Thompson, Frederick Douglass, and Samuel May, who put five fugitive slaves on the stage and demanded resistance to the law, inviting President Fillmore to do his worst. Fillmore, another New Yorker, visited Syracuse with his entire cabinet to let the abolitionists know that the government would enforce the Fugitive Slave Law. Daniel Webster thundered that "the Supreme Courts of the United States, New York and Massachusetts" all concurred that the law was constitutional and therefore must be obeyed.

It is within this context that we may understand the significance of Allen's reference to the Syracuse paper as a "Fillmore organ," and the anti-abolitionist newspapers' accounts of the mob violence against Mary King and William G. Allen under such headlines as "Another Rescue," the "Mary Rescue," and the "Fulton Rescue." These all referred to the famous "Jerry Rescue" in Syracuse during October 1851. Jerry McHenry, a mulatto born into slavery in North Carolina and sold in Missouri, escaped and settled in Syracuse. He was working in the shop of a member of May's church when a U.S. marshal and several deputies seized him, shackled him, and arrested him. He was legally a fugitive slave.

The Liberty Party convention was in progress and Gerrit Smith and others immediately appeared as Jerry McHenry's counsels. During the examination hearing May offered his church for the proceedings, and this apparently was a prearranged signal for the rescue. Black and white abolitionists crowded in to grab the fugitive, hoisted him above their heads, and passed him to the door. He was badly hurt during the rescue but, still shackled, he was put into a carriage. Deputies then recaptured him and took him to the police station. Samuel Ringgold Ward, the black abolitionist preacher, and Gerrit Smith walked arm in arm into City Hall while May and the others—including Jermain W. Loguen—met to plot further action. Samuel May wrote about the "Jerry Rescue"; Yacovone suggests that he was confused, to say the least, between his opposition to violence and his commitment to freeing Jerry McHenry from federal officers. Black abolitionists in Syracuse were not confused; Loguen said, "If white men won't fight, let fugitives and black men smite down Marshalls and Commissioners—any body who holds Jerry—and rescue him or perish." Some three thousand people eventually gathered to protest Jerry McHenry's capture; when the Whig *Syracuse Daily Standard* reported the incident, it inflated the crowd to ten thousand. Both blacks and whites stormed the police station. The rescuers shattered glass and hacked their way into the station; one marshal jumped out a second-story window. McHenry was finally rescued and hidden for five days before he was escorted across the border into Canada. He actually sued his captors the following year to test the Fugitive Slave Law's constitutionality, but the case went no further. Although May had every reason to believe that he would be tried for treason, he continued to support public resistance and he held annual "Jerry Celebrations" right up until the Civil War, attempting, he claimed, "to make Jerry McHenry's rescue as much a part of the nation's heritage as the Boston Tea Party." The *Syracuse Star* denounced May's rally and its speakers— Gerrit Smith, Garrison, Douglass, Lucy Stone, and Lucretia Mott—as "mob rule." The United States government continued attempts to prosecute the rescuers for nearly two years, with abolitionists staging rallies to raise funds for their defense well into 1853. These circumstances surely underlay the seemingly "private" courtship and engagement of William G. Allen and Mary King, and the white public's violent reaction to their attachment.

The Globe Hotel in Syracuse was known to house black guests but Allen, having just dropped in, had to depart quickly, about a week after the Fulton attack, while he was awaiting

CAUTION!!

COLORED PEOPLE
OF BOSTON, ONE & ALL,

You are hereby respectfully CAUTIONED and advised, to avoid conversing with the

Watchmen and Police Officers of Boston,

For since the recent ORDER OF THE MAYOR & ALDERMEN, they are empowered to act as

KIDNAPPERS
AND
Slave Catchers,

And they have already been actually employed in KIDNAPPING, CATCHING, AND KEEPING SLAVES. Therefore, if you value your LIBERTY, and the *Welfare of the Fugitives* among you, *Shun* them in every possible manner, as so many *HOUNDS* on the track of the most unfortunate of your race.

Keep a Sharp Look Out for KIDNAPPERS, and have TOP EYE open.

A handbill distributed in 1851 warned free blacks and fugitives in Boston about the new Fugitive Slave Law. Reprinted with permission of the Prints and Photographs Divisions of the Library of Congress.

Mary King. It took her several days to elude her parents and Fulton neighbors; Sarah and John Porter stayed in touch with Allen, in Syracuse, by mail. His letters to them had to be enclosed in a wrapper addressed to another man. Mary King's brother William attempted to lure him into a purported meeting with her near Fulton, but Allen, realizing the deception, adroitly refused the invitation. Finally, the *Syracuse Standard* carried Allen's own rebuttal to the anti-abolitionists' accounts. William King also published his version, although anonymously, claiming that Mary had rejected Allen's proposal of marriage not once but three times and that "Madame Gossip" was responsible for the rumor that they were engaged. Allen's response to this falsehood is, of course, that the proof of his account is that they married, and he includes excerpts from Mary King Allen's smuggled note written to him during their last few days in upstate New York. She arranged to meet him in Syracuse, at Loguen's, telling him, "I love you . . . yes, and I always shall until life's troubled waters cease their flow." They met in Syracuse at last, "at the house of a friend whose memory we hold in the highest reverence." We can only surmise that the friend was Loguen, an ally and friend of May's as well, and the real hero of the Jerry Rescue. Shortly thereafter *The Liberator* copied Allen's notice from the *Syracuse Standard,* whereupon it was read by Harriet Beecher Stowe, who wrote to Allen extending her sympathy, best wishes, and a copy of *Uncle Tom's Cabin.* If Alcott did not already know the details of William Allen and Mary King's travails from her uncle or from the New York papers, she certainly would have seen the account in *The Liberator,* which the Alcotts read faithfully.

Furthermore, Gerrit Smith, a congressional representative from New York, introduced a resolution at the Syracuse Liberty Party convention, which Samuel J. May attended: "Resolved— that the recent outrage committed upon that accomplished and worthy man—Professor William G. Allen—and the general rejoicing throughout the country therein, evinces that the heart of the American people, on the subject of slavery is utterly corrupt, and almost past cure."

Allen relates "something spicy": following newspaper reports of the Fulton case, a slaveholder in Mississippi wrote to Mr. King asking for permission to court Mary King; he had seen her the previous year when visiting the state of New York. He mentions the "Nine Young Negroes" in bondage to him and presents a list of six Southern gentlemen who would attest to his character, these including a senator, an ex-governor, a court clerk, a sheriff, and two editors.

Mary King went to Pennsylvania under the pretext of teaching school there, and wrote to Allen again professing her love and fiercely asserting her determination to join him: "should the public or my friends ever see fit to lay their commands upon me again, they will find . . . that woman is one who will never passively yield her rights. *They may mob me; yea, they may kill me; but they shall never crush me.*"

The couple then met by arrangement in New York City and was married there on March 30. They went on to Boston for ten days, staying with a friend, and from there took ship for Liverpool. Their faithful friend in New York, Mr. Porter, lost his job and wrote to the Allens that his next job ended after only three months, when it was discovered that he was the "Phillipsville School-master." Allen ends his narrative with a direct address, "Such, reader, is the character of prejudice against color,—bitter, cruel, relentless."

The Allens were well advised to choose England; Blackett meticulously traced their exile from 1853, when William Wells Brown's novel *Clotel* was published in London and *Uncle Tom's Cabin* was already a best-seller. Despite sincere efforts by notable British and Irish abolitionists, and the strenuous efforts of William Allen himself to earn a living by public lectures, the Americans did not prosper materially. Close to destitution several times, they ultimately had to appeal to Gerrit Smith for support. Mrs. E. Follen, an American married to a Harvard - professor, and Lady Byron proposed, as Blackett shows, that Allen lectured for the "Moral Reformatory School Movement"; Allen wrote that he hoped to follow a vocation that would render him "practically useful to the British public," and at the same time elevate him to "a position at once respectable and influential." But he was, as his biographer suggests, an academic and an intellectual, not a fiery orator or preacher. He wrote to *The Liberator*, the *Anti-Slavery Watchman*, *Anti-Slavery Reporter*, Frederick Douglass's paper, and eventually the British papers as well, urging that immigrants not adopt the American prejudice against color. His visits to Ireland at first augured well— the Anti-Slavery Society there successfully hosted Frederick Douglass, Charles Lennox Remond, and Henry Highland Garnet. In both Ulster and Dublin, his pure diction, his gentlemanly manner, and his erudition impressed Allen's audiences.

Mary and William Allen then moved to Dublin in 1856, and three of their seven children were born in Ireland. But lectures and private lessons did not bring enough income for them to survive. They returned to London, where British abolitionists were planning a free labor colony in Nigeria to compete with American slave-grown cotton. Allen, once an opponent of colonization, was finally persuaded that Liberian colonization might work. By 1863 Allen's ties to British philanthropists and reformers finally led to his directorship of the New Caledonian Training School in Islington, North London. He was the first man of color to direct a school in England. Five years later, however, he wrote to antislavery friends in Britain that an increase in rent and competition from other local schools had forced him out. He referred to the almost certain racism of his competitors as an influence "by a spirit not usually supposed to exist among Englishmen." From then on the story is increasingly sad. Mary King Allen started a small school for girls, which failed, and by 1878 the family, living in a boardinghouse in West London, were dependent on the charity of friends. Allen's letters, still held in the British and Foreign Anti-Slavery Society Papers, tell us these particulars. Brackett finds no record of the Allens in the English Register of Deaths and no trace of their ever returning to America. Mary King Allen and William G. Allen surely kept their pledges of loyalty and love to one another, but the "American Prejudice against Color" grew only more virulent in their lifetime.

WHAT MISCEGENATION IS!

—AND—

WHAT WE ARE TO EXPECT

Now that Mr. Lincoln is Re-elected.

By L. SEAMAN, LL. D.

WALLER & WILLETTS, Publishers,

The title page from a racist pamphlet published in 1864. The fear depicted is that free African Americans in the United States would naturally want social equality, which meant race mixing or *miscegenation,* the new term coined to replace the older term *amalgamation.* Reprinted with the permission of the Prints and Photographs Division of the Library of Congress.

Both Lincoln and Douglas used fears of amalgamation to win votes; in their famous debate Lincoln contended that "there is a natural disgust in the minds of nearly all white people to the idea of an indiscriminate amalgamation of the white and brown races." He carefully distinguished between antislavery and social integration, saying that he protested against the idea that the Declaration of Independence meant intermarriage between black and white. The fact that he did "not want a black woman for a slave" did not mean that he would "necessarily want her for a wife. I need not have her for either; I can just leave her alone. In some respects she certainly is not my equal; but in her natural right to eat the bread she earns with her own hands without asking leave of any one else, she is my equal and the equal of others."

Lincoln's election may have prompted the invention of the new word *miscegenation*. A pamphlet purporting to be pro-abolition and pro-amalgamation was written by David Goodman Croly and George Wakeman, editor and writer for the Democratic *New York World*, in 1863. Actually an anti-abolitionist hoax, it suggested the new term *miscegenation* as a combination of the Latin words *miscere,* to mix, and *genus,* race. *Amalgamation,* they said, was properly a metalworker's term for the union of compatible metals, while the new word was more precise and scientific. The pamphlet was popular, and its message was quickly absorbed. Horace Greeley used the word in the pro-abolitionist *New York Tribune,* and in the succeeding Darwinian discourses it has all but replaced the older term. Neither William G. Allen nor Mary King ever used the word *miscegenation.*

A Note on the Texts

The American Prejudice against Color reprints two pamphlets written by William G. Allen and a story written by Louisa May Alcott. The sources for these texts are as follows:

The American Prejudice Against Color. An Authentic Narrative, Showing How Easily the Nation Got into an Uproar. By William G. Allen, a Refugee from American Despotism. London: W. and F. G. Cash; Edinburgh: John Menzies; and Dublin: James McGlashan and J. B. Gilpin, 1853.

A Short Personal Narrative, by William G. Allen, (Colored American,) Formerly Professor of the Greek Language and Literature in New York Central College. Resident for the Last Four Years in Dublin. Dublin: 1860.

"M.L.," by Louisa May Alcott. Originally published in serial form in the *Commonwealth* 1, nos. 21, 22, 23, 24, and 25 (January 24, 31, February 7, 14, and 21, 1863).

In preparing these texts for publication I have made emendations only where the texts would be obviously unclear or erroneous without them. I have corrected spelling and typographical errors, inserted punctuation marks for clarity, and added missing single or double quotation marks. Nineteenth-century spellings and inconsistencies in punctuation and capitalization have been let stand as in the originals; in general, I have tried to "correct" these texts as little as possible.

References

Alcott, Louisa May. "M.L." *Commonwealth* 1, nos. 21, 22, 23, 24, 25 (January 24, 31, February 7, 14, 21, 1863). (Reprinted in *Journal of Negro History* 14, no. 4 [October 1929], and in *Louisa May Alcott on Race, Sex, and Slavery*, edited by Sarah Elbert [Boston: Northeastern University Press, 1997]).

Allen, William G. *The American Prejudice Against Color. An Authentic Narrative, Showing How Easily the Nation Got into an Uproar.* London, 1853.

———. *A Short Personal Narrative.* Dublin, 1860.

Bentley, Nancy. "White Slaves: The Mulatto Hero in Ante-Bellum Fiction." In *Subjects and Citizens*, edited by Michael Moon and Cathy Davidson. Durham, N.C.: Duke University Press, 1995.

Blackett, R. J. M. *Beating against the Barriers: The Lives of Six Nineteenth-Century Afro-Americans.* Ithaca: Cornell University Press, 1989.

———. *Building an Antislavery Wall: Black Americans in the Atlantic Abolitionist Movement, 1830–1860*. Ithaca: Cornell University Press, 1989.

———. "William G. Allen, the Forgotten Professor." *Civil War History* 26 (March 1980): 39–52.

Boyer, Paul S. *Urban Masses and Moral Order in America, 1820–1920*. Cambridge: Harvard University Press, 1978.

Brodkin, Karen. *How Jews Became White Folks and What That Says about Race in America*. New Brunswick: Rutgers University Press, 1998.

Brown, William Wells. *Clotel: or, The President's Daughter*. London, 1853.

Davis, David Brion. *From Homicide to Slavery: Studies in American Culture*. New York: Oxford University Press, 1986.

———. *Slavery and Human Progress*. New York: Oxford University Press, 1984.

"Ellis Gray Loring, 1803–1858." Obituary and commentaries on his life and works in *The Liberator*, May, June 4, 18, 1858.

Foner, Philip S., and George E. Walker, editors. *Proceedings of the Black State Conventions, 1840–1865*. Vol. 2. Philadelphia: Temple University Press, 1980.

Gilje, Paul. *The Road to Mobocracy: Popular Disorder in New York City, 1763–1834*. Chapel Hill: University of North Carolina Press, 1987.

Green, Beriah, to Gerrit Smith. "Whitesboro, Dec. 1840." In Gerrit Smith Papers, George Arents Research Library, Syracuse University. (Professor Milton Sernett, Department of African American Studies, Syracuse University, generously shared his work in progress, and this and other documents related to Allen's life and work.)

Hodges, Graham Russell. *Root and Branch: African Americans in New York and East Jersey, 1613–1863*. Chapel Hill: University of North Carolina Press, 1999.

Horton, James Oliver. *Free People of Color: Inside the African American Community*. Washington, D.C.: Smithsonian Institution Press, 1993.

Horton, James Oliver, and Lois E. Horton. *Black Bostonians: Family Life and Community Struggle in the Antebellum North*. New York: Holmes & Meier, 1979.

———. *In Hope of Liberty: Culture, Community and Protest among Northern Free Blacks, 1700–1860*. New York: Oxford University Press, 1997.

Kaplan, Sidney. "The Miscegenation Issue in the Election of 1864." *Journal of Negro History* 31 (July 1949): 274–343.

Kerber, Linda. "Abolitionists and Amalgamators: The New York City Race Riots of 1834." *New York History* 48 (1967).

Kinney, James. *Amalgamation! Race, Sex, and Rhetoric in the Nineteenth-Century American Novel.* Westport, Conn.: Greenwood, 1985.

Leach, William R. *True Love and Perfect Union: The Feminist Reform of Sex and Society.* New York: Basic Books, 1980.

Lemire, Elise Virginia. "Making Miscegenation: Discourses of Interracial Sex and Marriage in the United States, 1790–1865." Ph.D. dissertation, Rutgers, State University of New Jersey, 1996. (I am grateful to Professor Lemire for generously sharing her study with me before its publication.)

Lincoln, Abraham. *Speeches and Writings, 1832–1858.* New York: Vintage, 1989.

Mabee, Carleton. *Black Education in New York State.* Syracuse: Syracuse University Press, 1979.

Myerson, Joel, Daniel Shealy, and Madeleine B. Stern. *The Selected Letters of Louisa May Alcott.* Boston: Little, Brown, 1987.

Nyong'o, Tavia. "What Was Amalgamation? The Case of William Allen and Mary King," Presentation at Whitney Humanities Center, Yale University, January 25, 2002.

Pease, William H., and Jane Pease. *Black Utopia: Negro Communal Experience in America.* Madison: University of Wisconsin Press, 1972.

———. *Bound with Them in Chains: A Biographical History of the Antislavery Movement.* Westport, Conn.: Greenwood Press, 1972.

Richards, Leonard L. *Gentlemen of Property and Standing: Anti-Abolition Mobs in Jacksonian America.* London: Oxford University Press, 1971.

Ripley, Peter C., editor. *The Black Abolitionist Papers.* 5 vols. Chapel Hill: University of North Carolina Press, 1985.

Roediger, David. *The Wages of Whiteness: Race in the Making of the American Working Class.* London: Verso, 1991.

Sernett, Milton. *Abolition's Axe: Beriah Green, Oneida Institute, and the Black Freedom Struggle.* Syracuse: Syracuse University Press, 1986.

———. *North Star Country: Upstate New York and the Crusade for African American Freedom.* Syracuse: Syracuse University Press, 2002.

Short, Kenneth R. "New York Central College." *Foundations* 5, no. 3 (1962).

Stauffer, John. "Beyond Social Control: The Example of Gerrit Smith, Romantic Radical." *American Transcendental Quarterly* 11, no. 2 (1997): 233–59.

———. *The Black Hearts of Men: Radical Abolitionists and the Transformation of Race*. Cambridge and London : Harvard University Press, 2002.

Stern, Madeleine B. *Louisa May Alcott: A Biography.* New York: Random House, 1995.

Stowe, Harriet Beecher. *Uncle Tom's Cabin*. Reprint, New York: Harper Classics, 1965.

Tanner, Kevin. "Mr. Smith Becomes an Abolitionist: Gerrit Smith and the 1835 Utica Riot." Research paper, Binghamton University, 2001. (Kevin Tanner generously shared his newspaper sources and accounts of the Utica riot.)

Washington, Margaret. *Sojourner Truth: Her Life and Times*. New York: Pantheon, forthcoming. (I am grateful to Professor Washington for her generous help in locating archival materials and for her scholarly insights.)

———, editor. *Narrative of Sojourner Truth*. New York: Vintage, 1993.

White, Barbara A. "Our Nig and the She-Devil: New Information about Harriet Wilson and the Bellmont Family." *American Literature* 65, no.1 (March 1993): 19–52.

Wilson, Harriet. *Our Nig: or, Sketches from the Life of a Free Black, in a Two-Story White House, North, Showing That Slavery's Shadows Fall Even There*. 1859. Reprint, New York: Random House, 1983.

Winks, Robin W. *The Blacks in Canada: A History.* New Haven: Yale University Press, 1971.

Wright, Albert Hazen. "Cornell's Three Precursors: I. New York Central College." *Studies in History: A Publication of New York State College of Agriculture,* no. 23 (1960).

Yacovone, Donald. *Samuel Joseph May and the Dilemmas of the Liberal Persuasion, 1797–1871*. Philadelphia: Temple University Press, 1991.

THE AMERICAN
PREJUDICE AGAINST COLOR

THE AMERICAN

Prejudice Against Color.

AN AUTHENTIC NARRATIVE,

SHOWING HOW EASILY THE NATION GOT

INTO AN UPROAR.

BY WILLIAM G. ALLEN,

A REFUGEE FROM AMERICAN DESPOTISM.

LONDON:

W. AND F. G. CASH, 5, BISHOPSGATE-STREET-WITHOUT.

EDINBURGH: JOHN MENZIES.

DUBLIN: JAMES MC. GLASHAN AND J. B. GILPIN

1853

PREFACE.

Extract of a letter from Hon. Gerrit Smith, of New York, Member of Congress, to Joseph Sturge, Esq., of Birmingham, England. (By permission of Mr. Sturge.)

"*Peterboro', New York, March 23rd,* 1853.

"I take great pleasure in introducing to you my much esteemed friend, Professor Wm. G. Allen. I know him well, and know him to be a man of great mental and moral worth. I trust, in his visit to England, he will be both useful and happy.

"Very truly, your friend and brother,
"GERRIT SMITH."

"Commending Professor Allen to the friends of the colored American citizens who are denied their rights in their own country, and wishing him every success in the object before him,

"I am, respectfully,
"*Birmingham, 6mo., 28d.,* 1853.   "JOSEPH STURGE."

"*Clapham, August 25th,* 1853.

"My dear Sir:—

"Your determination to spend some time in Great Britain, and to employ yourself, as opportunities occur, in giving lectures and delivering addresses upon American topics, including the social position of the free colored population—for which your education and personal experience eminently fit you—has given me sincere pleasure. I trust you will meet with ample encouragement from the friends of Abolition throughout the United Kingdom, to whose sympathy and kindness I would earnestly recommend you, and still more your heroic and most estimable lady.

"Believe me, most truly yours,
"Professor W. G. Allen   "GEORGE THOMPSON."

CONTENTS.

CHAPTER I.

INTRODUCTION

MANY persons having suggested that it would greatly subserve the Anti-slavery Cause in this country, to present to the public a concise narrative of my recent narrow escape from death, at the hands of an armed mob in America, a mob armed with tar, feathers, poles, and an empty barrel spiked with shingle nails, together with the reasons which induced that mob, I propose to give it. I cannot promise however, to write such a book as ought to be written to illustrate fully the bitterness, malignity, and cruelty, of American prejudice against color, and to show its terrible power in grinding into the dust of social and political bondage, the hundreds of thousands of so-called free men and women of color of the North. This bondage is, in many of its aspects, far more dreadful than that of the *bona fide* Southern Slavery, since its victims—many of them having emerged out of, and some of them never having been into, the darkness of personal slavery—have acquired a development of mind, heart, and character, not at all inferior to the foremost of their oppressors.

The book that ought to be written, *I* ought not to attempt; but if no one precedes me, I shall consider myself bound by necessity, and making the attempt, lay on, with all the strength I can possibly summon, to American Caste and skin-deep Democracy.

The mob occurred on Sabbath (!) evening, January the 30th, 1853, in the village of Phillipsville, near Fulton, Oswego County, New York. The cause,—the intention, on my part, of marrying a white young lady of Fulton,—at least so the public surmised.

CHAPTER II.

PERSONALITIES.

I AM a quadroon, that is, I am of one-fourth African blood, and three-fourths Anglo-Saxon. I graduated at Oneida Institute, in Whitesboro', New York, in 1844; subsequently studied Law with Ellis Gray Loring, Esq., of Boston, Massachusetts; and was thence called to the Professorship of the Greek and German languages, and of Rhetoric and Belles-Lettres of New York Central College, situated in Mc. Grawville, Cortland County,—the only College in America that has ever called a colored man to a Professorship, and one of the very few that receive colored and white students on terms of perfect equality, if, indeed, they receive colored students at all.

In April, 1851, I was invited to Fulton, to deliver a course of Lectures. I gladly accepted the invitation, and none the less that Fulton had always maintained a high reputation for its love of impartial freedom, and that its citizens were highly respected for their professed devotion to the teachings of Christianity.

I am glad to say, that on this occasion I was well received, and at the close of my first lecture was invited to spend the evening at the house of the Rev. Lyndon King. This gentleman having long been known as a devoted abolitionist,—a fervid preacher of the doctrine, that character is above color,—and as one of the ablest advocates of the social, political, and religious rights of the colored man, I, of course, had a pleasant visit with the family; and, remaining with them several days, conceived a deep interest in one of the Elder's daughters,—Miss Mary E. King, who was then preparing to enter the College in Mc. Grawville. I accompanied Miss King to Mc. Grawville, where she remained in college, a year and a half.

Boarding in tenements quite opposite each other, we frequently met in other than college halls, and as freely conversed,—Miss K. being of full age, and legally, as well as intellectually and morally, competent to discuss the subjects in which, it is generally supposed, young men and women feel an absorbing interest.

It is of no consequence what we said; and if it were, the reader, judging in the light of the results, will perhaps as correctly imagine that, as I can possibly describe it. I pass on at once, therefore, simply stating that at the close of the year and a half, my interest in the young lady had become fully reciprocated, and we occupied a relation to each other much more significant than that of teacher and pupil.

Miss King returned to her father's house in October, 1852. I visited the family in December following. Then and there we discussed the subject of marriage more fully between ourselves; and deeming it a duty obligatory upon us, by an intelligent regard for our future happiness, to survey, before consummating an engagement even, the whole field of difficulties, embarrassments, trials, insults and persecutions, which we should have to enter on account of our diversity of complexion, and to satisfy ourselves fully as to our ability to endure what we might expect to encounter; we concluded to separate unengaged, and, in due season, each to write to the other what might be the results of more mature deliberation. This may seem unromantic to the reader; nevertheless, it was prudent on our part.

After remaining in Fulton a week, I left for Boston. Several letters then passed between us, and in January last, our engagement was fixed. I will not speak of myself, but on the part of Miss King, this was certainly a bold step. It displayed a moral heroism which no one can comprehend who has not been in America, and who does not understand the diabolical workings of prejudice against color. Whatever a man may be in his own person,—though he should have the eloquence, talents, and character of Paul and Apollos, and the Angel Gabriel combined,—though he should be as wealthy as Crœsus,—and though, in personal appearance, he should be as fair as the fairest Anglo-Saxon, yet, if he have but one drop of the blood of the African flowing in his veins, no white young lady can ally herself to him in matrimony, without bringing upon her the anathemas of the community, with scarcely an exception, and rendering herself an almost total outcast, not only from the society in which she formerly moved, but from society in general.

Such is American Caste,—the most cruel under the sun. And such it is, notwithstanding the claims set up by the American people, that they are Heaven's Vicegerents, to teach to men, and to nations as well, the legitimate ideas of Christian Democracy.

To digress a moment. This Caste-spirit of America sometimes illustrates itself in rather ridiculous ways.

A beautiful young lady—a friend of mine—attended, about two years since, one of the most aristocratic Schools of one of the most aristocratic Villages of New York. She was warmly welcomed in the highest circles, and so amiable in temper was she, as well as agreeable in mind and person, that she soon became not only *a* favorite, but *the* favorite of the circle in which she moved. The *young gentlemen* of the village were especially interested in her, and what matrimonial offer might eventually have been made her, it is not for me to say. At the close of the second term, however, she left the school and the village; and then, for the first time, the fact became known (previously known only to her own room-mate) that she was slightly of African blood. Reader,—the consternation and horror which succeeded this "new developement," are, without exaggeration, perfectly indescribable. The people drew long breaths, as though they had escaped from the fangs of a boa constrictor; the old ladies charged their daughters, that should Miss —— be seen in that village again, by no means to permit themselves to be seen in the street with her; and many other charges were delivered by said mothers, equally absurd, and equally foolish. And yet this same young lady, according to their own previous showing, was not only one of the most beautiful in person and manners who had ever graced their circle, but was also of fine education; and in complexion as white as the whitest in the village. Truly, this, our human nature, is extremely strange and vastly inconsistent!

Confessedly, as a class, the quadroon women of New Orleans are the most beautiful in America. Their personal attractions are not only irresistible, but they have, in general, the best blood of America in their veins. They are mostly white in complexion, and are, many of them, highly educated and accomplished; and yet, by the law of Louisiana, no man may marry a quadroon woman, unless he can prove that he, too, has African blood in his veins. A law involving a greater outrage on propriety, a more blasphemous trifling with the heart's affections, and evincing a more contemptible tyranny, those who will look at the matter from the beginning to the end, will agree with me, could not possibly have been enacted.

Colonel Fuller, of the *"New York Mirror,"* writing from New Orleans, gives some melancholy descriptions—and some amusing ones too—of the operations of this most barbarous law.

One I especially remember. A planter, it seems, had fallen deeply in love with a charming quadroon girl. He desired to marry her; but the law forbade. What was he to do? To tarnish her honour was out of the question; he had too much himself to seek to tarnish hers. Here was a dilemma. But he was not to be foiled. What true heart will be, if there be any virtue in expedients?

> "———In love,
> His thoughts came down like a rushing stream."

At last he got it. A capital thought, which could have crept out of no one's brain, save that of a most desperate lover. He hit upon the expedient of extracting a little African blood from the veins of one of his slaves, and injecting it into his own. The deed done, the letter of the law was answered. He made proposals, was accepted, and they were married,—he being willing to risk his caste in obedience to a love higher and holier than any coventionalism which men have ever contrived to establish.

O, Cupid, thou art a singular God! and a most amazing philosopher! Thou goest shooting about with thy electrically charged arrows, bringing to one common level human hearts, however diverse in clime, caste, or color.

Let not the reader suppose, however, that the white people of America are in the habit of exercising such honor towards the people of color, as is here ascribed to this planter. Far from it.

The laws of the Southern States, on the one hand, (I allude not now to any particular law of Louisiana, but to the laws of the Slave States in general), have deliberately, and in cold blood, withheld their protection from every woman within their borders, in whose veins may flow but half a drop of African blood; while the prejudice against color of the Northern States, on the other hand, is so cruel and contemptuous of the rights and feelings of colored people, that no white man would lose his caste in debauching the best educated, most accomplished, virtuous and wealthy colored woman in the community, but would be mobbed from Maine to Delaware, should he with that same woman attempt honorable marriage. Henry Ward Beecher, (brother of Mrs. Stowe) in reference to prejudice against color, has truly said of the Northern people—and the truth in this case in startling and melancholy—that, "with them it is less sinful to break the whole decalogue towards the colored people, than to keep a single commandment in their favour."

But to return to the narrative. Miss King, previously to the consummation of our engagement, consulted her father, who at once gave his consent. Her sister not only consented, but, thanks to her kind heart, warmly approved the match. Her brothers, of whom there were many, were bitterly opposed. Mrs. King—a step-mother only—was not only also bitterly opposed, but *inveterately* so. Bright fancies and love-bewildering conceptions were what, in her estimation, we ought not to be allowed to indulge.

In passing, it is proper to say, that this lady, though not lacking a certain benevolence,—especially that sort which can pity the fugitive, give him food and raiment, or permit him at her table even,—is, nevertheless, extremely aristocratic of heart and patronizing of temper. This statement is made upon quite a familiar acquaintance with Mrs. King, and out of no asperity of feeling. I cherish none, but only pity for those who nurture a prejudice, which, while it convicts them of the most ridiculous vanity, at the same time shrivels their own hearts and narrows their own souls.

Mrs. King was at first mild in her opposition, but finally resorted to such violence of speech and act, as to indicate a state of feeling really deplorable, and a spirit diametrically opposed to all the teachings of the Christian religion—a religion which she loudly professed, and which assures us that "God is no respecter of persons."

I judge not mortal man or woman, but leave Mrs. King, and all those who thought it no harm because of my complexion, to abuse the most sacred feelings of my heart, to their conscience and their God.

CHAPTER III.

NOBILITY AND SERVILITY.

THE reader will doubtless and also correctly imagine that situated as Miss King has now been shown to be, she could not have experienced many very pleasant hours either of night or day,— pleasant so far as the sympathy of her numerous relatives and friends could serve to make them such. Fortunately, however she was not of that class whose happiness depends upon the smiles or the approbation of others earned at any cost—but upon a steady obedience to what in her inmost soul, she regarded as demanded by the laws of rectitude and justice.

That a young lady could break away without a struggle from the counsellors, friends and companions of her youth, is not to be expected. Miss King had her struggles; and the letter written to me by her on the consummation of our engagement evinced their character, and also her grandeur and nobility of soul:—

"I have endeavoured to solve, honorably, conscientiously and judiciously, the greatest problem of human life; and God and the holy angels have assisted me in thus solving. Friends may forsake me, and the world prove false, but the sweet assurance that I have your most devoted love, and that that love will strengthen and increase in proportion as the regard of others may diminish, is the only return I ask."

What vows I uttered in the secret chambers of my heart as I read the above and similar passages of that letter, let the reader imagine who may be disposed to credit me with the least aptitude of appreciating whatsoever in human nature is grand and noble, or in the human spirit, which is lovely, and true, and beautiful, and of good report.

Throughout the letter there was also a tone of gentle sadness—not that of regret for the course in contemplation,—but that which holily lingers around a loving heart, which, while it gives itself away, may not even lightly inflict the slightest pang upon other hearts to which it has long been bound by dearly-cherished ties.

But family opposition was not the only opposition which Miss King expected to, or did indeed encounter. Whoever sought to marry yet, and did the deed unblessed or uncursed of public praise or wrath? And aside from extraordinary circumstances, it is so pleasant to dip one's finger into a pie matrimonial.

The following paragraph of a letter written to me by Miss King a few days after I left her in December, amused me much,—it may possibly amuse the reader:—

"Professor,—You would smile if you only knew what an excitement your visit here caused among the good people of Fulton. Some would have it that we were married, and others said if we were not already married, they were sure that we would be; for they knew that you would not have spent a whole week with us if there had been no love existing between you and myself. Some of the villagers came to see me the day after you left, and begged of me, if *I were determined to marry you, to do so at once, and not to keep the public in so much suspense.*"

Friend, have you ever heard or read of anything which came nearer to clapping the climax of the ridiculous than this most singular appeal couched in the last clause of this quotation, to the benevolence of Miss King? Certainly, if anything could have come nearer, it would have been the act of a certain lady who, having heard during this selfsame visit that we were to be married on the morrow, actually had her sleigh drawn up to the door, and would have driven off to the Elder's to *"stop the wedding"* had not her husband remonstrated. It is true, this lady opposed the marriage, not on the ground of an immorality, but of its inexpediency considering the existent state of American sentiment; but then it is curious to think of what amazing powers she must have imagined herself possessed.

Public opposition however, soon began to assume a more decided form. Neighbours far and near, began to visit the house of Elder King, and to adopt such remonstrance and expostulation as, in their view the state of the case demanded. Some thought our marriage would be dreadful, a most inconceivably horrid outrage. Some declared it would be vulgar, and had rather see every child of theirs dead and buried, than take the course which, they were shocked to find, Miss King seemed bent to do. Some sillier than all the rest, avowed that should the marriage be permitted to take place, it would be a sin against Almighty God; and it may be, they thought it would call down thunder-bolts from the chamber of heaven's wrath, to smite us from the earth.

"There is no peace," saith my God, "to the wicked."—And surely, clearer exemplifications of this saying of Holy Writ were never had, than in the brain-teasings, mind-torturings and heart-rackings of these precious people, out of deference to our welfare. May they be mercifully remembered and gloriously rewarded.

It is proper to introduce to the reader at this point, our cherished friends,—Mr. and Mrs. Porter,—and to say at once, that words are not expressive enough to describe the gratitude we owe them, nor in what remembrance we hold them in the deepest depths of our hearts. They stood by us throughout that season of intended bloody persecution, turning neither to the right nor the left, nor counting their own interests or lives as aught in comparison to the friendship they bore us, or to their love of the principles of truth, justice and humanity. Amid the raging billows, they stood as a rock to which to cling.

We had known these friends for months, nay, for years. They had also been students in Mc. Grawville, but had subsequently married, and at the time of my December visit to Fulton were teachers of a School in Phillipsville,—where, it may be proper here to say, was located the depôt of the Fulton trains of cars.

Not only belonging to that class of persons, (rare in America, even among those who claim to be Abolitionists and Christians), persons who do not *profess* to believe merely, but really *do* believe in the doctrine of the "unity, equality, and brotherhood of the human race;" and who are willing to accord to others the exercise of rights which they claim for themselves; but, having also great purity of heart and purpose, Mr. and Mrs.

Porter did not, as they could not, sympathise with those whose ideas of marriage, as evinced in their conversation respecting Miss King and myself, never ascended beyond the region of the material into that of the high, the holy and the spiritual. Of all the families of Fulton and Phillipsville, this was the only one which *publicly* spoke approval of our course. So that, therefore it will be expected, that while those true hearts were friendly to us, they were equally with ourselves targets at which our enemies might shoot.

I have introduced Mr. and Mrs. Porter at this point, because, at this point, their services to us commenced. But for these faithful friends, Miss King would not have known whither to have fled when she found as she did, her own home becoming any other than a desirable habitation, owing to the growing opposition and bitter revilings of her step-mother, and the impertinent intermeddlings of others.

Thus far the opposition which Miss King had experienced, though disagreeable, had not become too much for the "utmost limit of human patience." Soon, however, a crisis occurred, in the arrival in Fulton, of the Rev. John B. King. This gentleman's visit was unexpected, and it is due to him to say, that he did not come on any errand connected with this subject; for until he arrived in Fulton, he did not know of the correspondence which had existed between his sister and myself. Though unexpected, his visit as already intimated, was fraught with results, which in their immediate influence, were extremely sad and woeful.

Mr. King was a Reform preacher, and had even come from Washington, District of Columbia, where he had been residing for the last two years, to collect money to build a church which should exclude from membership those who held their fellow-men in bondage, and who would not admit the doctrines of the human brotherhood. Just the man to assist us, one would have thought. But it is easy to preach and to talk. Who cannot do that? It is easier still to *feel*—this is humanity's instinct—for the wrongs and outrages inflicted upon our kind. But to plant one's feet rough-shod upon the neck and heels of a corrupt and controlling public sentiment, to cherish living faith in God, and, above all to crush the demon in one's own soul,—ah! this it is which only the *great* can do, who, only of men, can help the world onward up to heaven.

Mr. King had scarcely entered the house, and been told the story of our engagement, when he manifested the most unworthy and unchristian opposition. Unworthy and unchristian, since he frankly averred, that had I the remaining fourth Anglo-Saxon blood, he would be proud of me as a brother. He was bitter, not as wormwood only, but as wormwood and gall combined. He would not tolerate me as a visitor at his house, in company with his sister, unless I came in the capacity of driver or servant. A precious brother this, and a most glorious Christian teacher.

I have said that the arrival of this gentleman marked a crisis in the history of our troubles; and it did so in the fact that by the powerful influence which he exerted over his father, adverse to our marriage, and by the aid, strength and comfort which he gave to his step-mother; the Elder was at last brought to a re-consideration of his views, and to abandon the ground which he had hitherto maintained with so much heroism and valour.

I shall say no hard things of Elder King; now that the storm is over, I prefer to leave him to his own reflections, and especially to this one, which may be embodied in the following question,—*What is the true relation which a Christian Reformer sustains to public opinion?*

Had the Elder, supposing it to have been possible, assumed towards us a position more adverse than the one he did in this singular and unexpected change, the results could not, for the time being at least, have been sadder or more disastrous. How it affected the feelings of his daughter, the reader can well imagine, who will remember, that upon her father she had hitherto relied as upon a pillar of strength, and especially as her rock of refuge from the storms which beat upon her from without. Stricken thus, a weak spirit would have given up in despair; but not so with this heroic and noble-minded lady, upon whom misfortune seemed to have no other effect than to increase her faith in God.

Elder King now, not as hitherto out of his deference to the feelings of his wife, but of his own accord, averred that I should on no consideration whatever, be permitted to enter his house, to hold a conference with his daughter, providing said conference was to be promotive of our marriage. Miss King was compelled, therefore, to make an arrangement with Mr. Porter, by which our interviews should be held in his house when I should arrive, as I was expected to do so in a few days, from Boston. Strange to say, however, and paradoxical as it may seem, on the day on which I was expected to arrive in Fulton, the Elder himself took his daughter from Fulton to Phillipsville to meet me. I reached Phillipsville, on Saturday afternoon, January 29th, and, of course, was not advised of this altered state of things, until my arrival there—the Elder's change having taken place within a very few days previous.

The method which Elder King took to evince his hostility—his exclusion of me from his house—was extremely injudicious; and I have no doubt that he, himself, now sincerely regrets it. It excited to action the mob spirit which had all along existed in the hearts of the people, and was only awaiting the pretext which the Elder gave—the placing of me before the community, as a marauder upon the peace of his family. The mob, also, gave to the matter what the King family, evidently afterwards, greatly deplored—extraordinary notoriety. Elder King would certainly have displayed more worldly sagacity, to say nothing of Christian propriety, to have admitted me into his house as usual, where we could, all together, have reasoned the matter; and if prejudices could not have been conciliated, the Elder, at all events, by his previous acquaintance with my character, had every reason to suppose that I should have conducted myself as became a gentleman and a Christian. But so it is,—prejudice thus bewilders the faculties, and defeats the objects which it aims most to accomplish.

CHAPTER IV.

THE MOB.

————

HARDLY unlooked for by myself was this mob, especially after I had learned of the direction which "the subject" had taken in the family of Mr. King.

On Sabbath afternoon, January 30th, while Mr. and Mrs. Porter, Mrs. Porter's sister, Miss King, and myself, were enjoying ourselves in social conversation, a gentleman from the village of Fulton called at the residence of Mr. Porter, to give an account of events as they were transpiring in the village. This gentleman was decidedly opposed to "amalgamation," expressed the utmost surprise that Mr. Porter should for a moment suppose that God ever designed the inter-marriage of white and colored persons,—but he was, nevertheless, a man of friendly disposition,—and as a friend he came to Mr. Porter. *We were to be mobbed,*—so this gentleman informed us. He advised escape on the part of Mr. Porter and myself, otherwise the house would be demolished! All Fulton, since Saturday night, he informed us, had been in arms. Crowds of men could be seen in the streets, at every point, discussing the subject of our marriage, and with feelings of the most extraordinary excitement; and similar discussions, he added, had been held during the live-long night preceding, in all the grog shops and taverns of the village.

All sorts of oaths had been uttered, and execrations vented. Tar, feathers, poles, and an empty barrel spiked with shingle nails had been prepared for my especial benefit; and, so far as I was concerned, it must be escape or death. Mr. Porter was to be mobbed, he said, for offering me entertainment, and for being supposed friendly to our union. This friend did not understand the whole plan of the onslaught, but he gave sufficient information to justify us in surmising that no harm was intended to be inflicted upon Miss King, or any lady of the house.

Knowing the brutal character of prejudice against color, and knowing also that I was supposed to be about to commit the unpardonable sin, I confess, that though surprised to learn that the mob intended murder, yet I was not surprised to learn many of the details which this friend so kindly gave us.

Mr. Porter suggested that after supper, he and I should retire to a neighbour's house, he supposing that if the mob should be foiled in their attempt to get us into their hands, they would, after all, pass away, and thus the matter blow quietly over. The suggestion, however, was not carried into effect; for we had scarcely finished tea ere they (the mob) were down upon us like wild beasts out of a den.

We first observed some twenty men turning a corner in the direction of the house; then about thirty or forty more, and soon the streets were filled with men—some four or five hundred. In the rear of this multitude there was driven a sleigh in which, we rightly conjectured, Miss King was to be taken home.

From the statements of the leader of the mob—statements afterwards given to the public—it seems that a Committee, composed of members of the mob, and constituted by the mob, suggested before reaching the house that if we were still unmarried there should be no violence done, as they intended to carry off the lady. A portion of this Committee also made it their duty to gain access to the apartment where our company were sitting, and to inform us of the intentions of the assembled multitude below, while the remainder of the Committee endeavoured by speeches and reasoning to quiet the mob spirit, which soon after the assembling, began to reach its climax.

This Committee was composed of some of the most "respectable" men of Fulton—lawyers, merchants, and others of like position. The reader will doubtless think it strange that such men should be members of a mob; and so it would be, if prejudice against color were not the saddest of all comments upon the meanness of human depravity. In this, more than in anything else did the malignant character of this American feeling evince itself—that to drive me off or kill me, if need be, the "respectable" and the base were commingled, like—

"Kindred elements into one."

Men who, under other circumstances, would have been regarded as beneath contempt, the vulgar minded and vulgar hearted—with these, even Christians (so called) did not hesitate to affiliate themselves in order to crush a man who was guilty of no crime save that, having a colored skin, he was supposed to be about to marry a lady a few shades lighter than himself. O, the length and breadth, the height and depth, the cruelty and the irony of a prejudice which can so be little human nature.

But to the Committee again. This Committee declared themselves to us to be a self-constituted body. But whether self-constituted or otherwise, it matters not, since they were to all intents and purposes members of the mob—if not in *deed*, still in spirit and in heart. They meant no more than to save the honor of their village by preventing, if possible, bloodshed and death. They were not men of better principles than the rabble—they were only men of better breeding. I do them no injustice. The tenor of their discourse to us at the house of Mr. Porter, the spirit of an article published by one of their number a few days after in the *"Oswego Daily Times,"* and the statements of the mob-leader, clearly satisfy me that had we been married, they (the Committee) deeming that our marriage would have been a greater disgrace to their village than even bloodshed or death, would have left us to our fate—Miss King to be carried off, or perchance grossly insulted, and myself left, as the spiked barrel especially evinced, to torture and to death. That this Committee saved my life, I have no doubt; and I have publicly thanked them for the act. So I would be grateful even to the man who took deadly aim at me with his revolver, and only missed his mark.

Previous to the death which I was to suffer in the spiked barrel, I was to undergo various torturings and mutilations of person, aside from the tarring and feathering—some of these mutilations too shocking to be named in the pages of this book.

Mr. Porter, as I have already said, was also to be mobbed; but, as we afterwards ascertained, only to be coated with tar and feathers and ridden on a rail.

The leader of the mob subsequently averred that so decided was the feeling in Fulton, that in addition to the hundreds who, in person, made the onslaught, there were hundreds more in waiting in the village, who, it was understood between the two companies, were ready to join the onslaughting party at but a moment's warning. Indeed, Mrs. Allen now assures me that on her way home that evening, conducted by a portion of the Committee, she twice met crowds of men still coming on to join the multitudes already congregated at Mr. Porter's. One of the Committee, fearing that if all Fulton should get together, excited as the people were, there would be blood-shed in spite of all that could be said or done, entreated one of these crowds to go back. But, heeding him not; on the villains went, some of them uttering oaths and imprecations, some of them hurrahing, and many of them proceeding with great solemnity of step—these last doubtless being church-members; for the mob was not only on Sabbath evening, but it is a notorious fact which came out early afterwards, that the churches on that evening were, every one of them, quite deserted.

Reader, the life of a colored man in America, save as a slave, is regarded as far less sacred than that of a dog. There is no exaggeration in this statement—I am not writing of exceptions. It is true there are white people in America who, while the colored man will keep in what they call "his place," will treat him with a show of respect even. But even this kind of people have their offset in the multitudes and majorities—the populace at large who would go out of their way to inflict the most demon-like outrages upon those whose skins are not colored like their own!

I have before me at this moment recent American papers which contain accounts of the throttling of respectably-dressed colored men and women for venturing no further even than into the cabins of ferry boats plying between opposite cities; of colored ladies made to get out of the cars in which they had found seats—in cars in which the vilest loafer, provided his skin be white might sit unmolested; of respectable clergymen having their clothes torn from their backs, because they presumed to ask in a quiet manner that they might have berths in the cabins of steamers on which they were travelling, and not be compelled to lodge on deck; and lastly, of a colored man who was not long since picked up and thrown over-board from a steam boat, on one of the Western rivers, because of some affray with a white man—while all the bye-standers stood looking on, regarding the drowning of the man with less consideration than they would have done the drowning of a brute.

Knowing all these things, and knowing also the peculiarity of the circumstances which surrounded me on that Sabbath evening, the reader will not be surprised, that when I saw the dense multitude surrounding the house of Mr. Porter, I at once came to the conclusion that I should not be permitted to live an hour longer. I was not frightened—was never calmer—prepared for the worst, disposed of my watch and such other articles of value as I had about my person.

Mr. Porter was below stairs at the time the mob approached. Soon he came running up, introducing the Committee to whom reference has already been made. They at once addressed us. I do not remember their words,—the purport of the whole, however, was that death was intended for me, provided we had been married; and as it was, I could only escape it, by Miss King consenting to go with them, and by myself consenting to leave the village; and further, that there must be no delay by either party.

One of the Committee, in order to assure me of the terrible danger by which I was surrounded, drew back the window curtains and bade me look out. I did not do so, however, since it was not necessary that I should look out in order to feel fully convinced that there were men below, who had determined to degrade themselves below the level of the brutes that perish. Such cursings, such imprecations, such cries of "nigger," "bring him out," "d——n him," "kill him," "down with the house," were never heard before, I hardly think, even in America.

Of course, to have attempted to resist this armed mob of hundreds of men would have been preposterous. It would have been, so far as I was concerned, at least, to have committed myself to instant death. Compelled, therefore, to make the best of our unfortunate situation, Miss King consented to go with the Committee, and I to leave the village—she, however, taking care to assure me in a whisper, that she would meet me on the following day in Syracuse. The lady was now conducted by the Committee through the mob to the sleigh. Not a word was spoken by a single ruffian in the crowd. All were silent until the driver put whip to his horse, when a general shout was sent up, as of complete and perfect triumph.

"Mistaken souls!"

Having reached her father's house, one of the Committee addressed a speech to her, hoped that for the sake of her family, and the community, Miss King would relinquish all partiality for Professor Allen, advised her also to go around among the ladies of the village, and consult with them, and assured her that he would be glad to see her at his house; and at any time when she felt disposed to come, he would send a sleigh to bring her.

Nothing remarkable about this speech. But the tone in which it was delivered!—that cannot be put upon paper. The speaker evidently thought the young lady would receive it all as a mark of gracious favor, and as assuring her that though she had been "hand and glove" with a coloured man, he would nevertheless condescend to overlook it. He was dealing with the wrong woman, however; and he received such a reply to his harangue as only a virtuous indignation could have prompted.

The reader must also be informed that a double-sleigh load of able-bodied men followed close behind the one in which Miss King was taken home. What this movement meant, I am not able very satisfactorily to conjecture. I venture the opinion, however, that the good folks supposed their victim would jump out of the sleigh in which she was riding, if a good opportunity should offer, and run back to the Professor; and so this last load, no doubt, was put on as the rear-guard of the posse.

Now for myself. Miss King having left, and the mob having been informed that I was about to leave, they were somewhat quieted, but were far from being appeased. That portion of the

Committee that remained with me, thought there was danger yet; and so, indeed, there was, judging hideous noises, bitter curses and ruffianly demonstrations, to be any proper criterion. They still cried, "bring him out" and "kill him." The Committee thought the safety of the house required that I should be removed at once; so I having gotten together my hat, valise and other effects, they took me under their protection and conducted me to the village hotel.

While I was being conducted out of the door, all manner of speech was hurled at me—a bountiful supply of that sort of dialectics which America can beat all the world at handling. However, the main desire of the mob at this point seemed to have been to get a sight of me; so they arraigned themselves in a double file, while I was conducted through the centre thereof, somewhat after the fashion of a military hero—a committee man at each side, one in front and another behind. Having passed completely through the file, the scoundrels then closed in upon me; some of them kicking me, some striking me in the side, once on the head, some pulling at my clothes and bruising my hat, and all of them hooting and hallooing after a manner similar to that which they practised when they first surrounded the house of Mr. Porter.

At length we reached the hotel—a quarter of a mile distant. The Committee were about to conduct me into the front parlour, when one fellow patriotically cried out, "God d——n it, don't carry that nigger into the front door." A true Yankee that! I have a penny laid up for that fellow, if I should ever chance to meet him.

I was conducted into the back parlour of the hotel, as being the most secure. Still the mob were not appeased, and besides, their numbers had increased. They hung around the house. Some of them opened the windows half-way and tried to clamber through them into the parlour where I was; and at last they way-laid the outer doors.

The sort of curses they indulged in meanwhile, I need not describe again. They were essentially the same as they had hitherto vented, save that one or two of them growing a little humorous, cried out occasionally "a speech from Professor Allen"—putting a peculiar emphasis on the professor.

The Committee busied themselves in furnishing two sleighs in which I was to be conveyed away, and also in appeasing the more ruffianly part of the multitude with cigars and such other articles as they choose to call for at the bar of the hotel. One of the sleighs was stationed at the back door of the hotel, and the other about two miles from Fulton. The plan was that I should get into the former and be driven to the latter, in which I was to be taken post haste to Syracuse—a distance of about twenty-five miles. The mob, however, suspected some of the details of the plan, and consequently every time I appeared at the back door, they made a rush at me seeking to wreak their vengeance. I escaped their violence, however, by stepping adroitly out of the way. And, as the tavern keeper had assured them that if they attempted violence upon me while I was under his roof, they would do it at their peril, many of them left, and I, at last, succeeded in reaching the sleigh at the back door and was driven off in safety. The mob unable to overtake me, still shouted a last imprecation.

For this said Sleigh ride, I paid Six dollars, about £1. 4s.; so I was robbed, if not murdered.

I will now describe the leader of the mob—Henry C. Hibbard. I will do it in short. This man is a clumsy-fisted, double jointed, burly-headed personage, about six feet in height, with a countenance commingling in expression the utmost ferocity and cunning. Hibbard is not a fool—but a knave. He is essentially a low bred man, and vulgar to the heart's core.

Some idea of the calibre of the man may be had in the fact that in his published Article in defense of the mob, he makes use of such expressions as "g'hals," "g'halhood" and the like.

He has great perseverance of character as is evinced in the fact that though I was several days behind the time at which I was expected to arrive in Fulton, he or his deputies never failed to be daily at the Cars so as to watch my arrival, and thus be in season with the onslaught.

This man set himself up, and was indeed so received by the

Elder and Mrs. King as their friend, counsellor, and adviser. A confirmation this, of what I have already said about the commingling of the "respectable" and the base. His mobocratic movements, however, it is but just to say, were unknown to the Elder and his wife until after the onslaught had been made. Mrs. King however did not deprecate the mob until its history had become somewhat unpopular, by reason of many of the "respectable" men becoming ashamed at last that they had been found in such company as Hibbard's. And even the Elder himself, though he deprecated the mob, still characterized it as the "just indignation of the public."

Hibbard, I have already said, published a written defence of the mob. The article was headed *"The Mary Rescue."*—and a most remarkable document it was—remarkable, however, only for its intense vulgarity, its absurd contradictions, and its ridiculous attempts at piety and poetry.

Me, he describes as the "Professor of Charms" and "Charming Professor," once—the "tawney charmer."

Hibbard's article is not by me; and, if it were, its defilement is such that I could not be tempted to give it at length. Laughable and lamentable as the article is in the main, I still thank Hibbard for some portions of it, and especially for that one which substantiates the charge which I have brought against the "respectable men of Fulton." Thus ends the mob.

CHAPTER V.

DARK DAYS.

READER, I am now to describe the events of the two weeks which followed the Fulton onslaught; and I can assure you that language has yet to be invented in which to write in its fullness what, when the children of certain parents shall look back fifty years hence, they will regard as the darkest deeds recorded in the history of their ancestors.

Diabolical as was the mob, yet the shameful and outrageous persecution to which Miss King was subjected during those memorable weeks, at the hands of her relatives and the Fulton Community, sinks it (the mob) into utter significance. How the human beings who so outraged an inoffensive young lady can dare call themselves christians, is to me a mystery which I, at least, shall never be able wholly to explain.

I have already said that Miss King assured me on parting on Sabbath evening that she would meet me in Syracuse on the morrow. Accordingly I awaited at the depôt, on Monday afternoon, the arrival of the Fulton train of cars. But she did not appear, and, for the first time, the thought occurred to me that the Fulton people were determined to leave nothing undone by which to fill out their measure of meanness.

On Tuesday morning next, February 1st, the following article appeared in the "*Syracuse Star*"—one of the organs of the Fillmore Administration. It needs no comment of mine to instruct the reader as to the character of the paper which could publish such complete diabolism:—

"ANOTHER RESCUE."

"A gentleman from Fulton informs us that that village was the theatre of quite an exciting time, to say the least, on Sunday evening last. The story is as follows:—Rev. Mr. King, Pastor of a regular Wesleyan Methodist, Abolition, Amalgamation Church at Fulton, has an interesting and quite pretty daughter, whom, for some three or four years past, he has kept at School at that pink of a 'nigger' Institution, called the Mc. Grawville College, located South of us, in Cortland County. While there, it seems that a certain genuine negro connected with the Institution, called Professor Allen, (Professor Allen! bah!!) and herself became enamoured of each other, and thereupon entered into the requisite stipulation and agreements to constitute what is known to those interested in such matters, as an 'engagement' to be married. A little time since, the damsel went home to her Amalgamation-preaching parents, and made known the arrangements whereby their lovely daughter expected soon to be folded in the hymenean arms of anti-alabaster Sambo. The parents remonstrated and begged, and got the brothers and sisters to interpose, but all to no effect. The blooming damsel was determined to partake of the 'bed and board,' and inhale the rich odours, refreshing perfumes, and reviving fragrance which Mc. Grawville College teaching had pictured to her in life-like eloquence; and more than this, she would not remain in membership with the denomination that preaches but declines to practice, and sent in her resignation in due form of law. Whereupon, down from Mc. Grawville comes the blushing Allen, all decked in wedding garb, and on Sunday morn he half woke from ponderous sleep, and thought he heard playing on the air such sweet music,—

> ' "As are those dulcet sounds in break of day,
> That creep into the dreaming bridegroom's ear,
> And summons him to marriage!" '

"But evening came, and as the anxious couple could not have the nuptial rites celebrated under the Rev. father's roof, they withdrew to Phillips' tavern, on the West side of the river, and made preparations for the ceremonies. In the meantime the affair got whispered about the town, and the incensed populace to some five hundred strong made ready to 'disturb the meeting.' Several of the prominent citizens, fearing lest a serious row should follow, repaired to the marriage-home, and while some kept the riot down by speeches and persuasions, others gained admittance to the colors. Allen, on being asked if he was married, replied 'no,' but that he would be in a few minutes. He was remonstrated with, and told the consequences that would ensue—that he would be mobbed, and must leave town immediately. He responded that he knew what he was about, was a free man, in a free country, and should do as he pleased. By this time the outsiders could be held still no longer, and the window curtains being drawn, our hero 'saw and trembled,' and cried for mercy. The damsel didn't faint, but at once consented to go home, and was hurried into a sleigh and driven off, while Sambo under disguise and surrounded by Abolitionists, was hustled out of the crowd over to the Fulton house. The multitude soon followed, eager and raving to grab the 'nigger,' but after a little, he was got away from the house, by some sly comer, and hurried off to Syracuse in a sleigh, at the top of two-horse speed. Thus the black cloud avoided the whirlwind, and thus ended 'Another Rescue.' "

This article, abominable as it is, was copied either in whole or in part by nearly every pro-slavery organ throughout America in a few days after the mob—with glorifications at what they supposed to be my defeat; and some of the papers copied the article with regrets that I had not been killed outright. And, indeed, this same "*Syracuse Star*" in a few days after the publication of the above article did what it could to inflame the populace of Syracuse to inflict upon me violence and death.

Nor were the pro-slaveryites the only persons who gloated with delight over the Article published by the "*Star.*" Hundreds, and I think I am within the bounds of truth, when I say that thousands of men and women calling themselves Abolitionists and Christians, were especially rejoiced at my "defeat;" and expressed themselves to that effect, though using more guarded language than those who made no pretensions to a love of truth, justice, and humanity.

The article abounds in falsehood, though to serve its purpose it is certainly adroitly written. We had not intended to be married on the evening of the mob, so that not only is the speech which the Editor puts in my mouth false, but so also is his statement that we repaired to Phillips' Tavern to have the nuptial rites celebrated. The story of my seeing, and trembling and crying for mercy, is also equally false.

It is also worthy of note that every paper which copied the article, varied the details, in order to suit its specific locality. Some of the versions of the affair were extremely amusing.

One of the papers described the mob as having taken place at Syracuse, and the on-slaught as having been made upon us while the ceremony was about being performed, whereat Miss King fled in one direction, and I in another.

One Editor in furnishing his readers with the details thought it necessary to a completion of the picture to describe my personal appearance. He had never seen me—but no matter for that. He had seen the "*Star's*" report, and what that did not give him, his imagination could supply. So he at it; and the next morning I appeared in print as "a stout, lusty, fellow, six feet and three inches tall, and as black as a pot of charcoal." Reader, you would laugh to see me after such a description—of my height, at least.

The telegraphic wires were also put in demand, and in less than forty-eight hours after the occurrence of the mob, the terrific news had spread throughout the country that a "Colored man had attempted to marry a White woman!" And incredible as it may seem to Britons, this "horrid marriage" was for weeks, not only discoursed of in the papers but was the staple of conversation and debate in the grog shops, in the parlors, at the corners of the streets, and wherever men and women are accustomed to assemble; and during this time also my life was in danger whenever I ventured in the streets. The reader will get some idea of the state of things when I assure him that about a week after the mob, I had occasion to call at the Globe Hotel, Syracuse; and had not been in the house more than ten minutes before the landlord came to me and requested me to retire, as he feared the destruction of his house—the multitude having seen me enter, he said, and were now assembling about the building. I walked quietly out in company with a gentleman in a counter direction to the mob, and so escaped their wrath.

But to return to the narrative. On Tuesday afternoon (two days after the mob) I awaited again at the Syracuse depôt, the arrival of the Fulton train of cars; supposing it possible that I might meet Miss King. She did not make her appearance, and there was now not a doubt left on my mind as to the character of what was going on in Fulton. Just as I was on the point of turning away from the depôt, a gentleman came up behind me, tapped me on the shoulder, and bade me get out of the way as quickly as possible; for the Fulton mobocrats, he informed me, had sent up word by telegraph to certain persons in Syracuse to mob me, if I should be seen about the car house. This gentleman also added that some of these persons were about the car house, wishing to have me pointed out.

It seems, the Committee that visited us on the evening of the mob, had overheard Miss King assure me that she would meet me on the following day in Syracuse; and they, or others of our keepers, had not only determined that no such meeting should be held, but that the mobbing should be repeated if I attempted again to see her.

Just as I was about to enter my lodging house on my return from the depôt, whom should I espy but my friend Porter turning the corner and approaching me. Of course I was glad to see him; and our conversation, at once, turned upon Fulton and the events of the two preceeding days. He informed me, much to my surprise, for I had hardly supposed that tyranny would have gone so far, that on the night following the mob, the people of the village had risen up *en masse*, and in solemn meeting dismissed him from his school. Glorious America! Land of the Free!

Mr. Porter had committed no crime—nothing was charged against him, save that he had entertained us, and was known to be favorable to our union, or rather unfavorable to any interference in a matter which was of sacred right our own.

Mr. P. gave me no information with regard to Miss King, except that she was at home, and that in consequence of the extraordinary excitement she would probably be unable to get out of Fulton for several days to come.

He returned to Fulton the next morning, and three or four days after, I received from him the following letter. It is significant:—

"Gilberts' Mills, February 4th, 1853.

"Professor Allen,—

"Dear Friend:—

"I write you under very extraordinary circumstances. I have been obliged to leave the vicinity of Fulton, for a while at least. I am now stopping at A. Gilbert's. How long I shall stay here, I cannot tell.

"Mary (Miss King) I have not seen or heard from, for two days. All communications between her and Julia, (her sister—who was favorable to our union) and our family has been broken off—strictly prohibited; and Hibbard's house, on the hill, is the watch tower to guard Elder King's house against such dangerous invaders as ourselves.

"When I came from Syracuse that morning, Hibbard was at the depôt on the watch. In the afternoon I went up to the Elder's, and was met on the door-step and told not to deliver any messages or letters to Mary. Of course, I had none with me to deliver, and so I told Elder King. But I saw Mary in the presence of the family and Hibbard, and Mrs. Case and Mrs. Sherman, and such like—for Elder King's folks have a great many such sympathisers now.

"I wanted to say some things to her not in the presence of these strangers—so to speak—in the family; *but she told me that she was permitted to say no word to any one but in the presence of such companions as were appointed for her. I went away sad, for Mrs. King is trying to torment her soul out of her, by constant upbraidings and railings.*

"Yesterday morning Sarah (Mrs. Porter) started to go up to see her, not having seen her since the affair of the mob; but a cutter from Phillipsville whipped by her, and when she had got near the house, the cutter came back bringing Elder King, who told her that they thought it advisable to request her not to go to his house—that, in a word, *they were determined to prevent all communication between our family and Mary.* Sarah came back. In the meantime, a man came to see me—Mr. Case—to tell me that I must not go to Elder King's—*that I could not go there without getting hurt.* In fact, I had been that morning to Fulton early, to see the Editor of '*The Patriot;*' while I was going through the street, a lot of rowdies gathered together and yelled after me. The explanation is easy. When I came from Syracuse, the story went that I was plotting to get Mary off. And I can hardly forgive Elder King for putting the sanction upon this falsity, by excluding us from his house. That act of Elder King gave the multitude full swing. They have now full liberty to mob me; *and last night I came very near getting into their hands. About sunset they came over headed by Hibbard,* and while stopping at the tavern on the way—this side of the bridge—a man whipped up to Watson's on horseback, and gave me the wink. George Gilbert was at our room, (a lucky chance) and so I got under the buffalo, and Sarah sat on the seat, and so we rode down straight by them, and thus foiled them again. To-day I went back—packed up, and put my trunks in a neighbor's house, and then came down here with Sarah and Libbie. Thus it is. *Mary—God help her—is in prison,—that is, she is guarded.* Elder King has consented to just such arrangements as Mrs. King and Hibbard and some of the heartless, officious aristocrats of the village saw fit to propose. It cannot be helped. Mary will doubtless be used well, corporally—but oh, the torment of being confined with such despicable companions. I trust she will be brave; though I did hear yesterday morning that she was somewhat indisposed and was abed. Her eyes are inflamed.

"I left the vicinity not altogether out of personal fear, but because I knew that my presence kept up the excitement. Allen, *it is impossible for you to conceive what a convulsion this village of Fulton has been thrown into.* A regular siege and cannonading could hardly have raised a greater muss.

"Write to me soon. Enclose to G. Gilbert on the *outside* wrapper. I dared not send from Phillipsville yesterday.

"Keep cool; and do not blame Elder King more than you can help, for I expect he is forced into some things. How much he is to be forgiven on account of the dilemma into which he has got himself, let time decide. I do not wish to make his case worse.

"Yours in friendship,

"JOHN C. PORTER."

[The italics and parentheses of the above letter are mine.
I shall add no comment.]

On Saturday afternoon, Feb. 5th,—still in Syracuse,—I received a visit from Wm. S. King, Esq. This gentleman is also a brother of Miss King. His visit seemed to have about it at the outset somewhat of a stealthy character, and I confess I did not receive him with any great degree of cordiality. He came on an errand, he said. His sister desired to have an interview with me, and to that end she would meet me at the house of a friend about four miles from the village of Fulton. The journey to this friend's—hers of four miles and mine of twenty or more—he assured me must be conducted with the greatest possible secrecy; for should the Fulton people hear of it, the most disastrous results would follow. His sister was very ill, he said—was suffering intense anguish of mind—had been confined to her chamber with bodily ailings—had an eye also in a dreadful condition, the sight of which was in danger of being lost—still, her anxiety to see me was so great that she had entreated to be taken even in this condition to the place aforesaid mentioned.

I understood this brother at once. I was not to be trapped. I had read human nature (so I think the result will justify me in saying) to a much better purpose than he. I declined holding the interview at the time, on account, as I urged, of his sister's feeble health and excited state of mind—but would have no objection, I added, to such an interview some two or three weeks to come. He then urged me to write, assuring me that he would take the letter willingly. This also, I refused to do. So at last he left me with the understanding that upon the recovery of his sister's health, we should have an "interview."

Mr. King returned immediately to Fulton, and on the Monday following, I received by post a letter from Miss King. It was not in her own hand-writing—she was too ill to write, but it was dictated to her sister. Just as I expected, Miss King had found it necessary considering the influences against her, and that her relatives and the community would have left no means untried, however illegal or disgraceful to thwart her in her designs,—nay, would have sworn her into a lunatic asylum rather than to have permitted her to marry me—to consent that our engagement should be broken. This letter was to announce the fact, while at the same time, it gave as the reason—deference to the feelings of father and brothers.

Of course, I did not reply to the letter. As the *"Star"* says— I knew what I was about.

On Tuesday morning, February 8th, I published in the *"Syracuse Standard"* the following card:—

"TO THE PUBLIC.—FROM PROFESSOR ALLEN."

"So much has been said and written on the subject of the late affair at Fulton, that the Public by this time must have had nearly *quantum sufficit;* yet I deem it not improper on my own behalf to add a remark or two. I shall not undertake to describe in detail, the murderous outrage intended to be inflicted on a quiet and unoffending man—that is not of much consequence now.

"I wish now simply to show the public, that those who made the onslaught upon me on Sabbath evening, a week ago, acted no less like a pack of fools than a pack of devils; and this can be shown almost in a single word, by stating that the whole story of my intention of being married on the evening in question, or that I went to Fulton intending to consummate an affair of the kind at any period of my recent visit there, is a fabrication from the beginning to the end. The wretch who 'fixed up' just such a story as he thought would inflame the rabble to take my life, will yet, I trust, meet with deserved scorn and contempt from a community who, whatever may be their prejudice against my color, have, nevertheless, a high sense of what belongs to their own honor and dignity, and to the character and reputation of their village.

"I make this statement with regard to this matter of marriage, not because I regard myself as amenable to the public to state to them *whom* or *when* I shall marry, but that since so much has been said upon the subject, I am quite willing they should know the truth as it is. They are tyrants, and very little-hearted, and exceedingly muddy-headed ones at that, who will presume to take a matter of this kind out of the hands of the parties to whom it specifically belongs, and who are acting law-abidingly and honorably in the premises.

"Here then is the story. Read it. A band of several hundred armed men—armed, as I have been told, with an empty barrel spiked with shingle nails, tar, feathers and a pole, came down upon a certain house in Phillipsville, opposite Fulton, on Sabbath evening, a week ago, to kill or drive out a single individual, conducting himself in a quiet, peaceable manner, and that individual, too, in physical stature, one of the smallest of men,—and in physical strength, proportionably inferior! If this is not cowardice as well as villainy—and both of them double-refined—then, I ask, what is cowardice, or what is villainy? The malignity of the whole matter also is set in a clearer light, when it is remembered that this same individual has never injured one of his assailants, nor has it been charged upon him that in his life-time he has ever inflicted the slightest wrong upon mortal man, but who has striven to maintain an upright character through life, and to fight his way for long years through scorn and contempt, to an honorable position among men. Truly, this is a precious country! However, it is some consolation to know that 'God is just, and that his justice cannot sleep for ever.'

"A gentleman of Fulton writes an article on this subject, to the 'Oswego Daily Times,' of February the 3rd. The spirit of this gentleman's article dishonors his heart. So filled is he with a prejudice which an eminent Christian of this country has rightly characterized, as a 'blasphemy against God,' and a 'quarrel with Jehovah,' that he will not even deign to call me by name, to say nothing of the title which has been legitimately accorded me, but designates me as a 'colored man, &c.' The object of this writer in thus refusing to accord to me so cheap and common a courtesy is apparent, and as contemptible as apparent. Let him have the glory of it,—I pity him. Had I been a white man, he would not have so violated what he is such a stickler for—'the laws and usages of society.'

"In another place in his article, he describes me as the 'negro.' This is preposterous and ridiculous. Were I a negro, I should regard it as no dishonor, since men are not responsible for their physical peculiarities, and since they are neither better nor worse on account of them. It happens in this case, however, that so far from being a negro, three-fourths of the blood which flows in my veins is as good Anglo-Saxon as that which flows in the veins of this writer in the *'Times,'*—better, I will not say, of course.

"Something also is said in this article from Fulton about the 'course we' (the young lady and myself) 'were pursuing.' Now, as the several hundred armed men strong who came down upon me on Sunday night, and some newspaper Editors, and this gentleman in particular, and the public very nearly in general, have taken the matter of judging what this 'course we were pursuing' was, out of our own hands, I propose to leave it still further with them. They can guess at it, and fight it out to their heart's content.

"Something also is said by this gentleman about 'wholesome advice being given me'—but I did not hear it, that's all. Besides, I never take advice from those who can not tell the difference between a man and his skin.

"One gentleman—a true man—came to me, and expressed his deep sympathy for me, and his sorrow that I had been so wrongfully treated and shamefully outraged, and entreated me to regard with pity, and not with anger, the murderous wretches outside. This is the speech that I remember, and remember it to thank the friend for his manifestation of kind and generous emotions.

"This Fulton 'Committe man' also says that 'the colored man asked if he was to be left to be torn to pieces.' Beyond a doubt, I asked that question. It was certainly, under the circumstances, the most natural question in the world; for I had really begun to think that the fellows outside had the genuine teeth and tail.

"I close this Article. To the Committee who so kindly lent me their protection on that memorable night, I offer my thanks and lasting gratitude.

"To the poor wretches who sought to take my life, I extend my pity and forgiveness.

"As to myself—having in my veins, though but in a slight degree, the blood of a despised, crushed, and persecuted people, I ask no favors of the people of this country, and get none save from those whose Christianity is not hypocrisy, and who are willing to 'do unto others as they would that others should do unto them'—and who regard *all* human beings who are equal in character as equal to one another.

"Respectfully

"WILLIAM G. ALLEN"

Simultaneously with the above card, there appeared in the *"Syracuse Journal,"* the following Article. It is from the pen of Wm. S. King—the brother aforesaid mentioned. It is in spirit a most dastardly performance, more so, considering that the gentleman really *did* know the circumstances, than anything which had hitherto been sent to the press. As a history of the "affair," it is almost a falsity throughout—and especially is it so in that part of it which describes Miss King as repulsing me with her abhorrence of the idea of amalgamation. I do not propose, however, to be hard on Mr. King. His untruthful and cowardly spirit has been sufficiently rebuked by the marriage which took place in less than two months after the publication of his article:—

"THE FULTON RESCUE CASE."

"Since the occurrence of the circumstances which induced the mob and consequent excitement at Fulton, on the 30th of last month, we have made considerable effort to procure a full and precise statement of the facts in the case. This we have finally succeeded in doing from a gentleman of standing, who is well acquainted with all the circumstances. They are as follows:—

"For some years past, Miss King has been attending the School at Mc. Grawville, known as the 'New York Central College,' in which Allen, the colored Professor alluded to, is one of the teachers.

"During that time, Allen became deeply interested in the lady, and proposed marriage to her. This she at once rejected, declaring that the thought of such a connection was repulsive to her.

"For some time after this, the Professor said no more upon the subject; but in the course of a year or so, *again* proposed marriage, and was *again* rejected.

"Thus matters stood until some time since, when Miss King left the School, and returned to her home in Fulton. Shortly after, Allen went to that place and called on her, and, after a short interview, again, for the third time, proposed marriage. She *again rejected him,* and told him *that such was her firm and fixed decision.* Her manner towards him, however, during all this period, had been kind and friendly, but she had always expressed her abhorrence of the idea of 'amalgamation.'

"By this time Madam Gossip had set the rumor afloat, that Allen and Miss K. were engaged to be married. Such a report was, of course calculated to produce a great excitement wherever it went.

"Allen, however, was not to be baffled by his former ill success, and was determined, if possible, to make the report good. He, therefore, a few days after his last rejection, wrote to a gentleman residing in Phillipsville, opposite Fulton—who had formerly been a student in Mc. Grawville—that he intended making him a visit. As all the parties had been friends and acquaintances at School, Miss K. was invited to be present for the purpose of having a friendly visit. She accordingly called upon them on Saturday afternoon, and at their earnest solicitations consented to spend the Sabbath with them.

"In the meantime, it was whispered about that the Professor and Miss K. were there for the purpose of being married. This, the people of Fulton determined at once, should not be done in that town. They, therefore, assembled several hundred strong, and appointed a Committee to wait upon the party, which they accordingly did, and informed the Professor that he must leave town, and the young lady that she must go home, to which request they both acceded without hesitation.

"The above is, as we have been informed, a full and true statement of the affair which has created such an excitement throughout the country."

The reader will see that the article appears as an editorial—another evidence that it is "conscience that doth make cowards of us all."

Should Mr. King ever see this little book, and wonder how I found him out, I will simply inform him that I chanced to be in the neighborhood of the Journal Office, when he went in with his piece; and further, I have the guarantee of the Editor.

I now subjoin an extract of a note which I received from Miss King, on the afternoon of February the 12th:—

"Fulton, Friday Morning, Feb. 11th.

"Professor Allen,—

"Dearest and best-loved Friend:—

"I am much better this morning; and if I could only see you for a few hours, I am sure I should be quite well again. I have been trying to persuade father to let me go to Syracuse this morning and see you, but he thinks my health is not in a state to admit of it now, but has promised me faithfully that I may meet you at Loguens, on Tuesday of next week.

★　　★　　★　　★　　★

"Professor—When I saw that article in the *'Syracuse Journal,'* holding you up in such a ridiculous light, and laboring to make such false impressions upon the mind of the public, my soul was on fire with indignation.

★　　★　　★　　★　　★

"I need not tell you again that I love you, for you know that I do; yes, and I always shall until life's troubled waters cease their flow.

"All communications that I receive from, or send to, you, *are read by father;* for I am a prisoner, yes, a *prisoner;* and when you write to me—if you should before I see you—*you must say nothing but what you are willing to have seen.* I shall manage to send this note without having it seen by any one.

"When I see you, I will tell you how much I have suffered since I saw you last, and how much I still suffer.

★　　★　　★　　★　　★

"Ever yours,

"MARY."

[The italicising of the above is my own.]

This little note was the only communication which I had received from Fulton, containing any account of the doings of the King family, since the letter written to me by Miss King, announcing that our engagement must be broken. Though short, it was satisfactory. It assured me that Miss King,—though she could be persecuted—could not be crushed.

About the same time that I received the above note from Miss King, I also received the following from Rev. Timothy Stowe, of Peterboro', New York. How much I valued this friendly epistle coming, as it did, from one of the most devoted Christians in America, it is not possible for me to say:—

"Peterboro', February 8th, 1853.

"Dear Brother Allen:—

"I see by the papers, that you have been shamefully mobbed at Fulton. I write to let you know that there are some in the world who will not join the multitude who are trying to overwhelm you with prejudice.

$$\star \quad \star \quad \star \quad \star \quad \star$$

"Now do not be cast down. You, I trust, are not the man to cower at such a moment. Do not be afraid to stand up your whole length in defence of your own rights.

"Come and visit us without delay. Consider my house your home while here.

"Brother Smith sends you his love. Brother Remington wishes me to say that you have his confidence, and that he is your friend.

"Yours with kindest regards,
"TIMOTHY STOWE."

CHAPTER VI.

BRIGHTENING UP.—GRAND RESULT.

ACCORDING to the intimation in the note received from Miss King dated Feb. 11th, she met me—not however as she expected on Tuesday—but, on Wednesday of next week in Syracuse: and at the house of a friend whose memory we hold in the highest reverence.

The interview, as the parents and relatives of Miss King understood it, was to be held to the intent that Miss King might then and there in person, and by "word" more effectually than she could possibly do by writing, absolve herself from all engagement, obligation or intention whatsoever to marry me—now, hereafter, or evermore. This was their construction of the matter, and it was in the light of this construction that they essayed to grant the request—the granting of which Miss King made the condition on which she proposed to yield up her sacred right.

That the King family—determined as they were, law or no law, justice or no justice, Christianity or no Christianity; in short, at all events and all hazards, to prevent our union—should have granted this interview to Miss King convicts them of as great imbecility and folly as was their persecution of their victim. But so it is, the innocent shall not only not be cut down, but they who practice unrighteousness shall themselves be overtaken.

But to the interview. I should be glad to describe my feelings on first meeting Miss King after she had passed through that fiery furnace of affliction. But I desist. The "engagement," I have already said, displayed a moral heroism which no one can comprehend who has not been in America, but the passage through was more than sublime.

She related to me the events of the two preceding weeks as she had known them to transpire in her own family, and as she had heard of them as transpiring in the village. I cannot write the details. It chills my blood to think of them. The various letters published in this narrative will suffice to give the reader some idea of things as they were; while the hundreds of things which cannot be written and which, because of their littleness are the more faithful exponents of meanness, must be left to the reader to imagine as best he can. I say as best he can, since no Englishman can imagine the thing precisely as it was.

She was reviled, upbraided, ridiculed, tormented; and by some, efforts were made to bribe her into the selling of her conscience. What the vilest and most vulgar prejudices could suggest were hurled at both our devoted heads. Letters were not permitted to be received or sent without their being first inspected by the parents. And finally she was imprisoned after the manner set forth in the letter of Mr. Porter. So rigid was the surveillance that her sister was also put under the same "regimen," because her sympathies were with the persecuted and not the persecutors.

When we met, therefore, we were not long in determining what was our duty. And now, Reader, what would you have done? Just what we did—no doubt. Made up your mind to have sacrificed nothing upon the altar of a vulgar prejudice. Such was the nature of the demand—would it not have been base to have yielded?

We concluded that now, more than ever, we would obey our heart's convictions, though all the world should oppose us; that, come what would, we would stand by each other, looking to Heaven to bless us, and not to man, for either smiles or favor.

We were resolved, but there was a difficulty yet. Determined to exercise our God-given rights, we were still overpowered by the physical force of the whole community. An open declaration by either party of our resolve would have been not less than consummate madness. To exercise our rights, therefore, not as we *would* but as we *could*, was the only hope left us.

We resolved to marry and flee the Country. Miss King returned to Fulton; after remaining there a week or ten days she went to Pennsylvania *ostensibly* to teach in a school. We corresponded by means of a third person; and my arrangements being made, we met in New York City, on March 30th, according to appointment; were married immediately and left for Boston. In Boston, we remained ten days, keeping as quiet as possible, in the family of a beloved friend, and on the 9th of April, took passage for Liverpool.

Since our arrival in this Country, we have received several American papers. The following Article is from one of the Western New York papers, which is but a specimen of the articles published by all the pro-slavery papers throughout the land on the announcement of the marriage, shows that the flight to England completed the victory. To have remained to be killed would have been fun to be relished. But public sentiment abroad—ah, that is another thing, and not so pleasant to be thought of:—

"PROF. ALLEN IS MARRIED"

"MARRIED.—In New York city, March 30th, by Rev. Thomas Henson, Professor WILLIAM G. ALLEN, of Mc. Grawville, N.Y., and Miss MARY E. KING, of Fulton, N.Y., daughter of Rev. Lyndon King, of Fulton.

"We expected as much. We were liberally abused for our discountenance of this marriage, and charged with wilfully falsifying facts, because we insisted that this affair was in contemplation, and would yet go off. *Prof.* Allen denied it, and others thought that they had the most positive assurance from his statements that the amalgamation wedding was a fiction. But now, after he and his white brethren have liberally impugned our motives, charged falsehood upon us, and made solemn asseverations designed to make the public believe that no such thing was in contemplation, in two brief months, the thing is consummated, with all the formality of a religious observance, and this unholy amalgamation is perpetrated before high Heaven and asserted among men.

"*Prof.* ALLEN and his fair bride are now in Europe. It is well they should emigrate, to show admiring foreigners the beauties of American abolitionism. Let them attend the receptions of the Duchess of Sutherland, the soirees of English agitators, and the orgies of Exeter Hall. Let GEO. THOMPSON introduce them as the first fruits of his *philanthropic* labors in America. Let them travel among the starveling English operatives, who would gladly accept slavery if assured of a peck of corn each week; let them wander among European serfs, whose life, labor, and virtue are the sport of despots, compared to whom the cruelest slave driver is an angel—and there proclaim their 'holy alliance.' If the victims of English and Continental tyranny do not turn their backs, disgusted with the foul connection, their degradation must be infinitely greater than we had supposed."

But to return to the story: Soon after the "interview" between Miss King and myself, I received the following note from Mrs. Harriet Beecher Stowe—the renowned Authoress of "Uncle Tom's Cabin." A "divine-hearted woman," this, as Horace Mann hath rightly called her, and more precious than rubies to me is her kind and Christian epistle:—

Andover, Massachusetts, February 21st, 1853.
"Professor Allen,—
 "Dear Sir:—
  "I have just read with indignation and sorrow your letter in the Liberator (copied from the Syracuse Standard). I had hoped that the day for such outrages had gone by. I trust that you will be enabled to preserve a patient and forgiving spirit under this exhibition of vulgar and unchristian prejudice. *Its day is short.*
 "Please accept the accompanying volume as a mark of friendly remembrance from,—

"H. B. STOWE."

Just before Miss K. left Fulton for Pennsylvania, she received the following letter from the Rev. Timothy Stowe—the gentleman to whom reference has already been made. He is not related to Mrs. Harriet Beecher Stowe, but is nevertheless of royal race:—

"Peterboro', New York, March 1st, 1853.
"Miss Mary E. King,—
"Dear Friend:—
"You will not be offended that I should address you by this title, though I never saw you, to my recollection, until last July at Mc. Grawville; I then felt an interest in your welfare—an interest which has been deepened by your recent insults and trials. I am not one of those who can censure you for your attachment and engagement to Professor Allen. He is a man—a noble man—a whole man; a man, in fine, of whom no woman need be ashamed. I am aware, you are aware, that the world will severely condemn you; so it did Luther, when he married a nun; it was then thought to be as great an outrage on decency, for a minister to marry a nun, as it now is for a white young lady to marry a colored gentleman. You have this consolation, that God does not look upon the countenance—the color of men; that in his eye, black and white are the same; and consequently, to marry a colored person of intelligence and worth is no immorality, and in his eye, no impropriety. It is probably the design of Providence in this case, to call the attention of the public to the fresh consideration of what is implied in the great doctrine of human brotherhood. Is it true or not, that a colored man has all the rights of a white man? Is this a question still mooted among Abolitionists? If so, then we may as well settle it now as at any other time, and though the controversy may be, and must be a very painful one to your feelings, yet, the result will be a better understanding of the great principles of our common nature and brotherhood. Professor Allen is with me in my study, and has detailed to me the whole of this outrage against yourself and him, and has also made me acquainted with your relations to each other. I extend to you my sympathy, I proffer to you my friendship. You have not fallen in my estimation, nor in the estimation of Mr. Smith and others in this place. Lay not this matter to heart, be not cast down; put your trust in God, and he will

bring you out of this crucible seven times purified. He in mercy designs to promote your spiritual growth and consolation. Keep the Saviour in your heart. My good wife sympathises with you. We would be glad to see you at our humble home, either before or after your marriage. We would try to comfort you; we would bear your burdens, and so 'fulfil the law of Christ.'

"Yours, with fraternal and Christian affection,

"Timothy Stowe."

On the day after Miss King left for Pennsylvania, I received the following note from a friend in Fulton. It is significant, and certainly corroborative of the opinion which I have expressed of the Fulton people—that they had determined to leave nothing undone by which to make their tyranny complete:—

"Fulton, March 5th, 1853.

"Dear Friend:—

"Yesterday I heard from you by a friend

    ★   ★   ★   ★   ★

"Mary has gone to Pennsylvania.

    ★   ★   ★   ★   ★

"What we feared was, she would be again imprisoned, and hindered from going to Pa. If her relatives and other friends knew of your intentions, she would have been put under lock and key as sure as there are *mean men* in Fulton.

    ★   ★   ★   ★   ★

"Professor, they were as mad as wild asses here about that 'resolution of Smith's,' especially King's folks.

    ★   ★   ★   ★   ★

I want your miniature—*must have it.* I want to show it to my friends that they may see this man whose idle moments in the bower of love sets half the world crazy.

★　　★　　★　　★　　★

"In friendship, yours,

"★　　★　　★"

The Resolution to which reference has been made, is as follows. It was presented by the Hon. Gerrit Smith, Member of Congress, from New York, at a Convention of "Liberty Party Men," held in Syracuse, about four weeks after the mob:—

"Resolved,—That the recent outrage committed upon that accomplished and worthy man—Professor William G. Allen—and the general rejoicing throughout the country therein, evinces that the heart of the American people, on the subject of slavery is utterly corrupt, and almost past cure."

Now for something spicy. The following letter was written to Elder King by a Slaveholder of Mississippi, about five weeks after the mob. The Elder re-mailed it to his daughter while she was in Pennsylvania. Having become the property of the daughter, and the daughter and I now being one, I shall take the liberty of giving this specimen of Southern chivalry to the public. The reader shall have it without alteration:—

"Warrenton, Mississippi,
"March 5th, 1853.

"Rev. Sir:—

"You cannot judge of my surprise and indignation, on reading an Editorial in one of my papers concerning an intending marriage of your lovely and accomplished daughter, with a negro man; which thanks to providence has been prevented by the excited and enraged populace of the enterprising citizens of the good town of Fulton.

"During my sojourn in the state of New York last year, I visited for mere curiosity the Mc. Grawville Institute in Cortland

85

Co., which gave me an opportunity of seeing your daughter, then a pupil of that equality and amalgamated Institute; and I believe in all my travels north, I never saw one more interesting and polite to those of her acquaintances.

"I have thought much about your daughter since my return home, and do yet, notwithstanding the ignominious connection she has lately escaped from. Your daughter—innocent, as I must in charity presume—because deluded and deranged by the false teachings of the abolition Institute at Mc. Grawville.

"My object in writing to you this letter is to obtain your permission to correspond with your daughter if it should be agreeable with herself, for I do assure you that I have no other than an honorable intention in doing so.

"I reside in Warren County near Warrenton—am the owner of Nine Young Negroes in agriculture, who would not exchange their bondage for a free residence in the north. I am happy to inform you Revd. Sir that my character is such that will bear the strictest investigation, and my relations respectable. I am yet young having not yet obtained my 25th year.

"Well sir, I am a stranger to both yourself and interesting family, and as a matter of course you may desire to know something about the humble individual who has thought proper to address you on a subject which depends on the future happiness of your daughter. For your Reverence's gratification you are at liberty to refer to either or all of the following gentlemen, by letter or in person,—viz., Hon. J. E. Sharkey, State Senator, Warren Co., P. O., Warrenton, Miss.;—Hon. A. G. Brown, Ex-Gov., Miss., now Member of Congress, P. O., Gallatin, Miss.;—Samuel Edwards, High Sheriff, Warren Co., P. O., Vicksburg, Miss.;—E. B. Scarbrough Clerk, Probate Court, Warren Co., P. O., Vicksburg, Miss.;—M. Shannon, Editor, Vicksburg, Miss., Whig;—Geo. D. Prentice, Editor, Louisville, Ky., Journal;—and Reed, Brothers, and Co., 177, Market Street, Philadelphia.

"Again Rev. Sir, I assure you that in writing you this letter, I only do that which is the result of mature deliberation.

"I shall wait anxiously your reply,

"THOS. K. KNOWLAND."

"P. S.—As Messrs. Reed, Brothers, and Co., are the nearest reference to whom I refer, I enclose you a letter from them."

The two letters immediately following were received by Miss K. just before she left Pennsylvania for New York. Many other letters were also received by both of us, which are not given in this book, but we can assure the writers thereof that they have our hearts' gratitude:—

"Fulton, March 27th, 1853.
"My dear and brave Sister:—

"For two weeks past we have been stopping with Mr. B. Yesterday we received four letters—two from my good brother B., and two from Pennsylvania, yours and Jane's. Right glad were we to receive those welcome favors—those little *epistolary* angels, telling us of your safety, (for safety has of late become quite a consideration) of your affection, of your anxiety, and a hundred things more than what were written.

"Mary, I judge from your letters and notes—from the tone of them—that there are feelings and emotions in your heart utterly beyond the power of words to express. You are resolved, and you are happy in your resolve, and strong in the providential certainty of its success. Yet you tremble for probabilities, or rather for *possibilities.*

"What feelings, dear Mary, you must have in the hour of your departure from this country. Through the windows of imagination I can catch a glimpse of it all. Your flight is a flight for freedom, and I can almost call you *Eliza.* To you this land will become a land of memory. And, oh! what memories! But we will talk of this hereafter.

"The remembrance of *friendship unbroken here,*—oh, Mary, let it not vanish as the blue hills of your father-land will dim away in the distance, while you glide eastward upon the 'free waters.' But let that bright remembrance be embodied in *spirit-*form, for ever attending you, and pointing back to those still here who hold you high in affection and in honor.

★   ★   ★   ★   ★

"Mary, I must close. Be firm—strong—brave—unflinching—*just like* Mary King.

"Yours in the bonds of love,
"JOHN C. PORTER."

"Fulton, March 27th, 1853.

"My dear Sister Mary:—

"Almost hourly since you left has your image been before me. And as I seat myself to write, thoughts and emotions innumerable come crowding for utterance. Gladly would I express them to you, dear Sister, but the pen is far too feeble an instrument. Oh, that I could be with you in body as in spirit. You need encouragement and strength in this hour; and I know that you will receive them,—for you are surrounded by a few of the truest and dearest of friends. And you know and have felt, that a higher and stronger power than earth can uphold us in every endeavour for the right.

★   ★   ★   ★   ★

"Mary, do you remember the time when you told me that I must love you better than I had ever done before; for friends would forsake you, and there would be none left to love you but P., and myself, and your father, and Julia, and J. B., and D. S., and S. T.? Our arms were twined around each other in close embrace. Your heart was full to overflowing, and words gave place to tears. I shall not forget the intense anxiety I felt for you at that moment as I tried to penetrate the future, knowing, as I did, somewhat of the cruelty of prejudice. It seems we both had a foreboding of something that would follow. I do not know that I wept, but heaven witnessed and recorded the silent, sacred promise of my heart to draw nearer and cherish you with truer fidelity as others turned away. And so shall I always feel.

★   ★   ★   ★   ★

"Oh, Mary, how little can we imagine the sufferings of the oppressed, while we float along on the popular current. I thank God from the depths of my soul, that we have launched our barks upon the ocean. Frail they are, yet, having right for our beacon, and humanity for our compass, I know we shall not be wrecked or go down among the raging elements.

*   *   *   *   *

"Now, dear Sister, farewell, and as you depart from this boasted 'land of liberty and equal rights,' and go among strangers, that you may, indeed, enjoy liberty, be not despondent, but cheerful, ever remembering the message of your angel mother.

*   *   *   *   *

Again, dear sister, farewell,—you know how much we love you, and that our deepest sympathies are with you wherever you may be.

"Affectionately yours,
"SARAH D. PORTER."

I subjoin an extract of a letter which I received from Miss K. a few days before our marriage:—

"Dolington, Pennsylvania
"March 21st, 1853.

"Professor Allen,—

"Dearest and best-loved Friend:—

"I have just received your letter of March 13th, and hasten to reply.

"You ask me if I can go with you in four weeks or thereabouts. In reply, I say yes; gladly and joyfully will I hasten with you to a land where unmolested, we can be happy in the consciousness of the love which we cherish for each other. While so far from you, I am sad, lonely, and unhappy; for I feel that I have no home but in the heart of him whom I love, and no country until I reach one where the cruel and crushing hand of Republican America can no longer tear me from you.

★　★　★　★　★

"Professor,—I sometimes tremble when I think of the strong effort that would be put forth to keep me from you, should my brothers know our arrangements. But my determination is taken and my decision fixed; and should the public or my friends ever see fit to lay their commands upon me again, they will find that although they have but a weak, defenceless woman to contend with, still, that woman is one who will never passively yield her rights. *They may mob me; yea, they may kill me; but they shall never crush me.*

"Heaven's blessings upon all who sympathised with us. I am not discouraged. God will guide us and protect us.

"Ever yours,

"MARY."

' "Thou Friend, whose presence on my wintry heart
Fell like bright Spring upon some herbless plain;
How beautiful and calm and free thou wert
In thy young wisdom, when the mortal chain
Of Custom thou did'st burst and rend in twain,
And walked as free as night the clouds among." '

Some idea of the spirit of persecution by which we were pursued may be gathered from the fact, that when the mobocrats of Fulton ascertained that Miss King and myself were having an interview in Syracuse, they threatened to come down and mob us, and were only deterred from so doing by the promise of Elder King, that he would go after his daughter if she did not return in the next train.

CHAPTER VII.

CONCLUSION.

READER,—I have but a word or two more to say.

Insignificant as this marriage may seem to you, I can assure you that nothing else has ever occurred in the history of American prejudice against color, which so startled the nation from North to South and East to West. On the announcement of the probability of the case merely, men and women were panic-stricken, deserted their principles and fled in every direction.

Indignation meetings were held in and about Fulton immediately after the mob. The following Resolution was passed unanimously in one of them:—

"Resolved,—That Amalgamation is no part of the Free Democracy of Granby." (Town near F.)

The Editor of the Fulton newspaper, however, spoke of us with respect. Let him be honored. He condemned the mob, opposed amalgamation, but described the parties thus,—"Miss King, a young lady of talent, education, and unblemished character," and myself, "a gentleman, a scholar, and a Christian, and a citizen against whose character nothing whatever had been urged."

I have said that some of the Papers regretted that I had not been killed outright. I give an extract from the *"Phoenix Democrat,"* published in the State of New York:—

"This Professor Allen may get down on his marrow bones, and thank God that we are not related to Mary King by the ties of consanguinity."

To show that I have not exaggerated the spirit of persecution which beset us, I will state that in a few days after Mr. Porter was dismissed from his School, he called upon the pastor of the church of which he is a communicant; and though without means—the chivalrous people who turned him out of his School not having yet paid him up—and knowing not whither to go, the pastor assured him that he could not take him in, or render him any assistance, so severely did he feel that he would be censured by the public.

That Mr. Porter is still pursued by this fiendish spirit, the reader will see by the following paragraph of a letter received from him a few days since:—

"I have advertised for a School in S——. They would not tolerate me in O——, after they found out that I was the Phillipsville School-master. I was employed in O—— three months."

Such, reader, is the character of prejudice against color,—bitter, cruel, relentless.

THE END.

A SHORT PERSONAL NARRATIVE

BY WILLIAM G. ALLEN

A SHORT

PERSONAL NARRATIVE,

BY

WILLIAM G. ALLEN,

(Colored American,)

FORMERLY

PROFESSOR OF THE GREEK LANGUAGE AND LITERATURE IN

NEW YORK CENTRAL COLLEGE

RESIDENT FOR THE LAST FOUR YEARS IN DUBLIN.

DUBLIN:

SOLD BY THE AUTHOR,

AND BY

WILLIAM CURRY & CO., 9, UPPER SACKVILLE-STREET, AND

J. ROBERTSON, 8 GRAFTON-STREET.

1860

PRICE ONE SHILLING.

DUBLIN: PRINTED BY ROBERT CHAPMAN,
TEMPLE LANE DAME STREET.

PREFACE.

In preparing this little narrative, I have not sought to make a book, but simply to tell my own experiences both in the slave-holding and non-slaveholding States of America, in as few words as possible. The facts here detailed throw light upon many phases of American life, and add one more to the tens of thousands of illustrations of the terrible power with which slavery has spread its influences into the Northern States of the Union—penetrating even the inmost recesses of social life.

W. G. A.

Donnybrook, Dublin,
 January, 1860.

A SHORT PERSONAL NARRATIVE.

I was born in Virginia, but not in slavery. The early years of my life were spent partly in the small village of Urbanna, on the banks of the Rappahannock, partly in the city of Norfolk, near the mouth of the James' River, and partly in the fortress of Monroe, on the shores of the Chesapeake. I was eighteen years in Virginia. My father was a white man, my mother a mulattress, so that I am what is generally termed a quadroon. Both parents died when I was quite young, and I was then adopted by another family, whose name I bear. My parents by adoption were both coloured, and possessed a flourishing business in the fortress of Monroe.

I went to school a year and a half in Norfolk. The school was composed entirely of coloured children, and was kept by a man of color, a Baptist minister, who was highly esteemed, not only as a teacher, but as a preacher of rare eloquence and power. His color did not debar him from taking an equal part with his white brethren in matters pertaining to their church.

But the school was destined to be of short duration. In 1831, Nathaniel Turner, a slave, having incited a number of his brethren to avenge their wrongs in a summary manner, marched by night with his comrades upon the town of Southampton, Virginia, and in a few hours put to death about one hundred of the white inhabitants. This act of Turner and his associates struck such terror into the hearts of the whites throughout the State, that they immediately, as an act of retaliation or vengeance, abolished every colored school within their borders; and having dispersed the pupils, ordered the teachers to leave the State forthwith, and never more to return.

I now went to the fortress of Monroe, but soon found that I could not get into any school there. For, though being a military station, and therefore under the sole control of the Federal Government, it did not seem that this place was free from the influence of slavery, in the form of prejudice against color. But my parents had money, which always and everywhere has a magic charm. I was also of a persevering habit; and what therefore I could not get in the schools I sought among the soldiers in the garrison, and succeeded in obtaining. Many of the rank and file of the American army are highly educated foreigners; some of them political refugees, who have fled to America and become unfortunate, oftentimes from their own personal habits. I now learned something of several languages, and considerable music. My German teacher, a common soldier, was, by all who knew him, reputed to be both a splendid scholar and musician. I also now and then bought the services of other teachers, which greatly helped to advance me.

Many of the slaveholders aided my efforts. This seems like a paradox; but, to the credit of humanity, be it said, that the bad are not always bad. One kind-hearted slaveholder, an army officer, gave me free access to his valuable library; and another slaveholder, a naval officer, who frequented the garrison, presented me, as a gift, with a small but well selected library, which formerly belonged to a deceased son.

My experience, therefore, in the State of Virginia, is, in many respects, quite the opposite of that which others of my class have been called to undergo.

Could I forget how often I have stood at the foot of the market in the city of Norfolk, and heard the cry of the auctioneer—"What will you give for this man?"—"What for this woman?"—"What for this child?" Could I forget that I have again and again stood upon the shores of the Chesapeake, and, while looking out upon that splendid bay, beheld ships and brigs carrying into unutterable misery and woe men, women and children, victims of the most cruel slavery that ever saw the sun; could I forget the innumerable scenes of cruelty I have witnessed, and blot out the remembrance of the degradation, intellectual, moral and spiritual, which everywhere surrounded me—making the country like unto a den of dragons and pool of waters—my reminiscence of Virginia were indeed a joy and not a sorrow.

Some things I do think of with pleasure. A grand old State is Virginia. No where else, in America at least, has nature revealed herself on a more munificent scale. Lofty mountains, majestic hills, beautiful valleys, magnificent rivers cover her bosom. A genial clime warms her heart. Her resources are exhaustless. Why should she not move on? Execrated for ever be this wretched slavery—this disturbing force. It kills the white man—kills the black man—kills the master—kills the slave—kills everybody and everything. Liberty is, indeed, the first condition of human progress, and the especial hand-maiden of all that in human life is beautiful and true.

I attained my eighteenth year. About this time the Rev. W. H—— of New York city visited the fortress of Monroe, and opened a select school. He was a white man, and of a kind and benevolent nature. He could not admit me into his school, nevertheless he took a deep interest in my welfare. He aided my studies in such ways as he could, and, on his return to the State of New York (he remained but a short time in Virginia), acquainted the Honorable Gerrit Smith, of Peterboro, with my desires. Mr. Smith's sympathies were immediately touched on my behalf. He requested the Rev. W. H—— to write to me at once, and extend to me an invitation to visit the State of New York, enter college, and graduate at his expense—if need be.

I have to remark just here that at the time of the visit of the Rev. W. H—— to the fortress of Monroe, my parents were in greatly reduced circumstances, owing to a destructive fire which had recently taken place, and burned to the ground a most valuable property. The fire was supposed to be the work of incendiaries—low whites of the neighbourhood, who had become envious of my parents' success. There was no insurance on the property. Under these circumstances I gladly accepted the kind offer of Mr. Smith. His generous nature then and there turned towards me in friendship; and, I am happy to be able to add, he has ever continued my friend from that day to this.

Mr. Smith is one of the noblest men that America has ever produced; and is especially remarkable for his profound appreciation of that sublime command of our Saviour, "All things whatsoever ye would that men should do to you, do ye even so to them." Where he treads no angel of sorrow follows.

He is a man of vast estates—a millionaire. He is also what in

America is termed a land reformer. He believes that every man should possess an inviolable homestead. He himself possesses by inheritance millions of acres in the Northern and Eastern States of America; and shows his sincerity and consistency by parcelling off from time to time such portions of these lands as are available, in lots of forty or fifty acres each, and presenting the deeds thereof, free of charge, to the deserving landless men, white or black, in the region where the lands in question are located. He also long since vacated the splendid Peterboro' mansion, into possession of which he came on the death of his father; and now resides, himself and family, in a simple cottage near Peterboro', with only forty acres attached. His sympathies are not bounded by country or clime. He sent into Ireland, during the famine of 1847, the largest single donation that reached the country from abroad.

He was elected to the United States Congress a few years ago, as one of the members for New York, but resigned his seat after holding it only a year—probably feeling outraged by the manners and morals, not to say superlative wickedness, of so many of his associates. Whatever may have been the cause which induced him to resign, he did well to give up his post. Nature had evidently not set him to the work. Of great ability, winning eloquence, and undoubted moral courage, his heart and temper were too soft and apologetic to deal with the blustering tyrants who fill too many of the seats of both houses of Congress.

Mr. Smith is truly a great orator. He has in an eminent degree the first qualification thereof—a great heart. His voice is a magnificent bass, deep, full, sonorous; and, being as melodious as deep, it gives him enviable power over the hearts and sympathies of men.

In personal appearance he is extremely handsome. Large and noble in stature, with a face not only beautiful, but luminous with the reflection of every Christian grace.

He is now engaged in the care of his vast estates, and in his private enterprises, scarcely private, since they are all for the public good. He is sixty-two years of age. A true Christian in every exalted sense of the term, long may he live an honor and a blessing to his race.

Having accepted the invitation of this gentleman, I prepared to leave the South. On making arrangements for a passage from Norfolk to Baltimore, I found that the "Free Papers" which every man of color in a slave state must possess, in order to be able to prove, in case of his being apprehended at any time, that he is not an absconding slave, were of very little avail. I must needs have a "Pass" as well, or I could not leave. However I obtained this document without much trouble, and as it is a curious specimen of American literature, I will give it. It does not equal, to be sure, the "charming pages" of Washington Irving, but it is certainly quite as illustrative in its way:—

"Norfolk, Oct. 1839.

"The bearer of this, William G. Allen, is permitted to leave Norfolk by the Steam Boat Jewess, Capt. Sutton, for Baltimore.

"Signed, J. F. Hunter
"Agent, Baltimore Steam Packet Company."

This document was also countersigned by one of the justices of the peace. Really, there is something preposterous about these slaveholders. They make all sorts of attempts to drive the free colored people out of their borders; but when a man of this class wishes to go of his own accord, he must that be *permitted!*

I reached Baltimore in safety, but now found that neither "Free Papers" nor "Pass" were of any further use. I desired to take the train to Philadelphia *en route* to New York. I must this time get a white man to testify to my freedom, or further I could not go. Or, worse still, if no such man could be found, I must be detained in Baltimore and lodged in jail! By no means a pleasant prospect. There was no time to be lost. My previous experience had taught me this truth—the more we trust, the more we are likely to find to trust. Acting upon this principle, and putting in practice my studies in physiognomy, I presently found a friend among the crowd; who, being satisfied with my statements and the documents I presented, kindly gave the desired testimony. The ticket seller then recorded my name, age, and personal appearance in his book, and delivered me my ticket. I now had no further trouble, and reached the college (in the State of New York) in safety.

Remaining at this college (Oneida Institute, Whitesboro') five years, I graduated with some honor and little cost to my patron, Mr. Smith. I quite paid my way by private tuitions: during one vacation I taught a school in Canada.

I cannot leave Oneida Institute without paying the tribute of my heart's warmest admiration and love to the President thereof—Reverend Beriah Green. America has few such men—men of that true greatness which comes from a combination of wisdom and virtue. Wherever found in that country, they are the "chosen few," consecrating their energies to the cause of Humanity and Religion—nobly and earnestly seeking to rid their country of its dire disgrace and shame. President Green still lives. He is a profound scholar, an original thinker, and, better and greater than all these, a sincere and devoted Christian. To the strength and vigor of a man, he adds the gentleness and tenderness of a woman. He has never taken an active part in the world of stir and politics; but in the line of his proper profession has immeasurably advanced the cause of human progress. May such men be multiplied in America, and elsewhere, for surely there is need.

Out now in the great world of America, my ambition was to secure a professorial chair. That any man having the slightest tinge of color, nay, without tinge of color, with only a drop of African blood in his veins, let his accomplishments be what they may, should aspire to such a position, I soon found was the very madness of madness. But something must be done. I repaired at once to the city of Boston, and entered the law office of E. G. L——, Esq. a distinguished barrister, who had already shown his regard for the colored race by having brought to the bar a colored young man—now practising with much success in Boston. Black men may practice law—at least in Massachusetts. I remained in the office of this gentleman two years, and was just entering my third and last year, when, unsolicited on my part and to my great surprise, I received the appointment of Professor of the Greek Language and Literature in New York Central College—a college of recent date, and situated in the town of M'Grawville, near the centre of the State of New York. This was the first college in America that ever had the moral courage to invite a man of color to occupy a professor's chair; and, so far as I know, it is also the only one.

The college was founded by a few noble-minded men, whose object was to combat the vulgar American prejudice, which can see no difference between a man and his skin. They sought to illustrate the doctrine of Human Equality, or brotherhood of the races; to elevate the nation's morals, and give it more exalted views of the aims and objects of Christianity. Such a college, in the midst of corrupt public sentiment, could not fail to meet with the greatest opposition. It was persecuted on all sides, and by all parties, showing how deep-seated and virulent is prejudice against color. The legislature countenanced the college so far as to grant it a charter, and empowered it to confer degrees, but would not, seemingly on no earthly consideration, give it the slightest pecuniary patronage. The debates which took place in the State House at Albany when the bill relating to the college came up for consideration, would, in vulgar flings at "negroes," cries of "amalgamation," and such like, have disgraced a very assemblage of pagans. However the college held on its way, and is still doing its work, though its efficiency is of course greatly marred. All the other professors were white; so also were the majority of the students.

———

I was four years in connexion with this college as professor, and in all probability would have been in M'Grawville still, but for the following circumstances.

I bethought me now of marriage, having what might be termed good prospects in the world. Visiting the town of Fulton, County of Oswego, State of New York, about forty miles from New York Central College, on an occasion of public interest, I was made the guest of the Rev. L. K——, a highly esteemed minister of the gospel, and greatly distinguished for his earnest and zealous advocacy of the principles of abolition. He was a white man. This gentleman had a large family of sons and daughters. A feeling of friendship sprung up between one of his daughters and myself on the occasion of this visit, which feeling eventually ripened into emotions of a higher and more interesting character. The father welcomed me: the mother was long since deceased. The parties immediately concerned were satisfied—why should others demur? I knew something of prejudice against color, but I supposed that a sense of dignity, not to say decency, would deter the most bitterly opposed from interference with a matter wholly domestic and private, and which, in its relation to the public, was also wholly insignificant. I reckoned without my host however. The inhabitants of Fulton had received the impression that there was an union in contemplation between the lady and myself; and they determined that it should not take place, certainly not in their town, nor elsewhere if they could prevent it. They stirred the town in every direction, evoking all the elements of hostility, and organizing the same into a deadly mob, to act at convenient opportunity. I was ignorant of the great length to which this feeling had attained; so also were the parties immediately interested in my personal safety. I was therefore greatly surprised when, on the occasion of my last visit to Fulton, and while in company with the lady, both of us visiting at the house of a mutual friend, residing about two miles out of town, a party rushed into our presence in hot haste, bidding me, if I wished to escape with my life, to "fly with all possible speed!" The party who performed this kindly office had scarcely gone, when, on looking out of the window, I beheld a maddened multitude approaching—about six hundred white men, armed with tar, feathers, poles and an empty barrel spiked with shingle nails! In this barrel I was to be put, and rolled from the top to the bottom of a hill near by. They also brought a sleigh, in which the lady was to be taken back to her father's house. They intended no harm to her.

Knowing the character of an American mob, and also knowing how little they value the life of a man of color, I expected, as I saw the multitude surrounding the house, to die—in fact, prepared for death.

Having assembled about the premises, they began to cry out in the most uproarious manner, "Bring him out!" "Kill the Nigger!" "Hang him!" "Tear down the house!" Shouts, groans, maledictions of all sorts and degrees followed. No one who has not witnessed an American mob can have the slightest idea of the scene which presented itself at this point. Had six hundred beasts of the forest been loosed together, in one promiscuous assemblage, they could scarcely have sent up howls and yells and mad noises equal to those made by these infuriated men. There is no exaggeration in this statement. For the sake of humanity, I only wish there was. Nor were the members of the mob confined entirely to the rabble; far from it. Many of its members were also members of a Christian church. The mob occurred on a Sabbath evening, about six o'clock, so that these men absolutely deserted their pews on purpose to enjoy the fun of "hunting the nigger."

There came with this mob a self-constituted committee of gentlemen, lawyers, merchants, and leading men of the town, who, although partaking of the general feeling of prejudice against color, did not wish, for the sake of the reputation of their town, to see bloodshed; besides also many of them, I doubt not, entertained feelings of personal friendship for myself.

This committee divided itself. One half came up to the drawing-room, and advised that the young lady should consent to go home in the sleigh provided, and that I should consent to leave the town. Conceding so much to the mob, they thought my life might be spared. The other half of the committee remained below, to appease the maddened multitude, and deter them from carrying their threats into execution.

We agreed to the propositions of the committee. The young lady was taken home in the sleigh aforesaid, about one third of the mob following on foot, for what purpose I know not. I was then conducted by the committee through the mob, many members of which giving me, as I passed, sundry kicks and cuffs, but doing me no serious bodily harm. I was next taken by the committee to an hotel, where arrangements had been made for my reception. The mob followed, hooting and hallooing, the sight of their victim seeming to revive their hostile feelings. They would have broken into the hotel, had not the proprietor held them back by his threats. He was not a friend of mine, but he had agreed to shelter me, and he was, of course, determined to protect his property.

The committee then secured the use of two sleighs, one of which they placed at the back entrance of the hotel, and the other they caused to be driven about four miles out of the town. Into the first sleigh I was to get when I could find my opportunity, and be driven to the other sleigh, in which I was to be finally conveyed to the town of Syracuse, about twenty-five miles distant. I made several attempts to get into the sleigh at the back entrance of the hotel, but was driven back by the mob every time I made my appearance at the door. Meanwhile the committee furnished the mobocrats with spirits to drink, and cigars to smoke, for all of which I had to pay. Comment upon this extraordinary act of meanness would be entirely out of place. One would have thought that these mobocrats would have been content to have mobbed me free of expense, at least. Not so it seemed however.

But midnight drew on, and of course the multitude grew weary. Presently, seeing my opportunity, I jumped into the sleigh at the back entrance of the hotel, drove rapidly off to the second sleigh, and reached the town of Syracuse early next morning. Some of the mobocrats attempted chase, but soon gave it up.

Had this tumult ended here, I should probably have been in my chair at the college today; and the whole affair, so far as it related only to myself, would have been regarded by me as merely a bit of an episode in my life—of course a most exciting one. But the worst was to come, at least so far as it concerned the lady personally; and the very worst it would be better to say nothing about.

After we had been disposed of in the manner already described, the next step taken by the inhabitants of the town of

Fulton was to place the lady under a most degraded surveillance. True, she was to continue in her father's house, but so overpowering had the mob-spirit become, that the mobocrats commanded (and were obeyed!) that no communications should be sent to her or from her, unless they had been previously perused and sanctioned by duly deputed parties. Nor would they permit any persons to call upon her, unless they too had been previously approved.

There was a line of railway between the towns of Fulton and Syracuse. Guards were placed by certain individuals at the various stations on the line, in order to prevent the possible escape of either party, or rather to prevent the possible meeting of the parties, *i.e.,* of the lady and myself. Meanwhile the telegraphic wires and newspapers spread the news throughout the length and breadth of the land; the consequence of all which was, I became so notorious that my life was placed in jeopardy wherever I went. On one occasion particularly I barely escaped with it.

On the day after the occurrence of the mob, and for several days after, the town of Fulton presented a scene of unparallelled excitement. Had the good people witnessed the approach of an invading army, but, by some lucky chance, succeeded in driving it back, they could not have been more extravagant in their demonstrations. Their countenances indicated the oddest possible mixture of consternation and joy. Seriously, if one can be serious over such details, never before did the contemplated marriage of two mortals create such a hubbub.

The inhabitants of Fulton immediately assembled *en masse,* and voted unanimously, in congress especially convened for the purpose, that Mr. and Mrs. P——, school teachers, our friends, at whose house we were being entertained at the time of the mob, "DO GIVE UP THEIR SCHOOL, AND LEAVE THE TOWN FORTHWITH." For what crime? None, save that of showing us hospitality. Our friends had therefore not only to give up their business at an immense pecuniary sacrifice, but had absolutely to make off with their lives as best they could.

During all this time the lady who had been thus rudely treated was true to her noble and heroic nature; but so much outward pressure, and of such an extraordinary character, produced its consequences upon her health. It failed, and it became necessary that she should be released from her thraldom. Once more at liberty she visited, incognito, the town of Syracuse, where I was still tarrying. The mobocrats would not have permitted her to have left Fulton in peace, if they had known whither she was going.

We met again: reviewed the past and discussed the future. As I am not detailing sentiment, but merely stating facts, suffice it to say, that we made up our minds that we would not be defeated by a mob.

But to the future. What was to be done? We came to the conclusion that I could no longer expect to hold my position in M'Grawville. The college had already received a terrible shock by reason of the cry of "amalgamation" which had been raised by the mob. And though the trustees were willing, at heart, to face the storm of prejudice, worldly wisdom, they considered, dictated that they should not incur the odium which they could not avoid bringing upon the college, if they persisted in retaining me longer as one of their professors. The trustees thought it would be better to be cautious, and save the college for the good it might do in the future. Such a union as ours was, in fact, but one of the logical results of the very principles on which the college was founded. I do not profess to sit in judgment, and therefore attempt no comment. They were now evidently anxious that I should resign, though, of course, they did not express so much to me in words.

I also came to the further conclusion that I could no longer, under the circumstances, whatever I might be able to do in future, hold my position in the country. For, however willing I might be to endure all things in my own person, I felt that I ought not to expose to any further danger one who already suffered so much and so heroically for my sake. I knew several of the lady's friends who were bitterly opposed to our union, solely on account of my color, and who were prepared, if the occasion should require it, to go to desperate lengths. They would not have hesitated to have sworn her into the lunatic asylum. I therefore decided not only to resign my professorship in the college, but also to leave the country.

Our plans being now quietly arranged, the lady returned to Fulton, and it was then supposed that all communication between us was for ever broken off. The mob had ordered that it should be so, and doubtless thought it was so. The most mistaken idea they ever entertained. The lady remained for a short time in Fulton, and then retired into the interior of the state of Pennsylvania. I continued to remain in the town of Syracuse.

Soon a favorable opportunity presented itself, and we met in the city of New York, on the 30th March, 1853, and then and there asserted our rights in due and legal form: after which we immediately took the train for Boston.

Owing to the great publicity which the newspapers had given to our affairs and the consequent excitement thereon, we found it necessary to use the utmost caution, such as walking apart in the streets, and travelling in the trains as strangers to each other. It would have been fool-hardy to have provoked another mob.

We remained in Boston ten days, quietly visiting among our friends, and then set sail for England. Wishing to get out of the country without farther ado, we were compelled to submit to many sacrifices, pecuniary and otherwise, of which it is not necessary to speak. In England and Ireland, including a short trip to Scotland, we have been ever since, and have constantly received that generous and friendly consideration which, from the reputation of Great Britain and Ireland, we had been led to expect; and for which we are grateful.

To go back for a single moment to New York Central College. On receiving the appointment to the professorial chair, the proslavery newspaper press of the country opened a regular assault. The *"Washington Union"* thus wrote:

"What a pity that college could not have found white men in all America to fill its professors' chairs. What a burning shame that the trustees should have been mean enough to rob Mr. L—— of his law student, and the Boston bar of its ebony ornament." I was never at the Boston bar, and therefore could not have been its ebony ornament. The imagination of the editors supplied them with the fact, and that answered their purpose as well.

A reverend doctor of divinity writing in a Cincinnati newspaper, wondered "how a man of sense could enter that amalgamation college. If this professor would go to Liberia and display his eloquence at the bar there; or, if he has any of the grace of God in his heart, enter the pulpit, he would then be doing a becoming work."

From Augusta, Georgia (Slave State), I received the following document, signed by several parties, and containing the picture of a man hanging by the neck, under which was written, "Here hangs the Professor of Greek!"

"Augusta, Geo. Nov. 1850.

"Sir,—We perceive you have been appointed Professor of Greek in New York Central College. Very well. We also perceive that you have occasionally lectured in the North on the 'Probable Destiny of the African Race.' Now, Sir, if you will only have the kindness to come to Augusta, and visit our hemp yard, you may be sure that your destiny will not be *probable*, but certain.

"Signed,

———
———
———"

Of course I did not go to Augusta, Georgia.

These assaults and attempts at ridicule served to bring me into general notice. I soon found that, by reason of them, and without merit or effort of my own, I had become known throughout the whole country as "the Colored Professor." I had a status. The lady being the daughter of a highly respectable minister, she also had a status. To permit therefore the union of these parties would be to bring the principle of amalgamation into respectability. So reasoned those who attempted to reason on behalf, or rather in excuse, of the mob. "We are sorry," they went on condescendingly to say, "for Professor Allen, for though a man of color, he is nevertheless a gentleman, a Christian and a scholar. But this union must not be; the 'proprieties of society,' must not be violated!" Here then was the secret of this extraordinary outbreak. Had we moved in what these good people would have been pleased to term a lower strata of society, they would have let us alone with infinite contempt.

The most lamentable feature of this Fulton mob was the fact, that we could not, if we had sought it, have secured any redress. No court of law in the State would have undertaken to bring to justice the perpetrators of this outrage. But on the contrary, such court would have been inclined to take sides with the mobocrats, and to justify them in the means which they employed wherewith to chastise a colored man who had presumed so grossly to violate the "proprieties of society."

Before closing I cannot forebear a further word with regard to New York Central College. During the four years I was in connexion with that college as professor, I never experienced the slightest disrespect from trustees, professors or students. All treated me kindly, so kindly indeed that I can truly say that the period of my professorship forms one of the pleasantest remembrances of my life. Terrible as prejudice against color is, my experience has taught me that it is not invincible; though, as it is the offspring of slavery, it will never be fully vanquished until slavery has been abolished.

In illustration of the direct influences of slavery as they affect the free man of color, I again go back for a single moment. Having spent three years at Oneida Institute, I proposed to myself a visit to Virginia, to look once more into the faces of beloved parents, relatives and friends, to walk again upon the strand at Fortress Monroe, where I had so often in childhood beheld the sunbeams play upon the coves and inlets, and seen the surf beat upon the rocks. I, at first, had some difficulty in getting a passage to Virginia, most of the masters of the New York vessels to whom I applied seeming to be of a friendly nature, and not willing to expose me to the slave laws of Virginia. I, however, succeeded at last—the captain of a Philadelphia vessel consenting to land me at the fortress of Monroe. I remained in the home of my childhood and youth seven days in peace; but on the morning of the eighth day, while walking on the strand, I was rudely assaulted by a person who had known me from my infancy. I had always supposed him to be a gentleman, and was therefore greatly surprised and shocked. But slavery is relentless; it ruins both the morals and the manners. This individual, after belaboring me in a savage manner, gave me distinctly to understand that unless I left Virginia speedily, I might find myself in trouble. He afterwards remarked, as I understood, to his friends that "this Allen has been off to an abolition college and returned among us. Let us look out for him."

I took the hint; and on the next morning secured the services of a party who rowed me off in a small canoe to a vessel lying in the harbor, where I bargained with the captain, who, for a handsome sum, consented to take me quietly out of the state. I left Virginia at once, and have never returned to it since, though I would gladly have done so, as relatives and friends near and dear to me have since died, by the side of whose death beds I desired to stand. In conclusion I have only to say that were I in the United States of America to-morrow, it would be more than my life or liberty would be worth to put foot upon the soil of my native state. Is this freedom? If it be, then give me slavery indeed.

A word or two with regard to my course in this country. Hitherto my income has been derived solely from lectures, tuitions, and such other odds and ends of work in my line as my hands could find to do. I desire a more permanent settlement for myself and family, and hope that the sale of this little narrative may help to create means to that end.

I send it forth therefore, desiring that it may stand upon its own merits, at the same time earnestly hoping that it may interest all into whose hands it may fall.

From LORD SHAFTESBURY.

"Lord Shaftesbury sympathizes most heartily with Professor Allen and sincerely wishes him success in his undertaking. It will give Lord Shaftesbury great pleasure to assist, in any way that he can, a gentleman of the colored race, who is a hundred times wiser and better than his white oppressors.

"LONDON, *July,* 1854."

From Rev. I. G. ABELTSHAUSER, LL.D. Trinity College, Dublin, and others;—

"DUBLIN, 14th April, 1856.

"The undersigned having made due enquiry from the most trustworthy sources relative to the character and attainments of Professor William G. Allen, have much pleasure in recommending him as a gentleman of high attainments and honorable character.

> I. G. ABELTSHAUSER, Clk. LL.D. Trin. Col. Dub.
> WM. URWICK, D. D. 40, Rathmines Road, Dublin.
> JAMES HAUGHTON, 35 Eccles-street, Dublin.
> RICHARD ALLEN, Sackville-street, Dublin.
> JONATHAN PIM, 22, William-street, Dublin.
> JOHN EVANS, M. D. 38, Richmond-street, Dublin.
> R. D. WEBB, 176, Great Brunswick-street, Dublin.
> JOHN R. WIGHAM, 36, Capel-street, Dublin.

From RICHARD D. WEBB, Esq. of Dublin.

"DUBLIN, 3rd November, 1858.

"DEAR MR. ALLEN,

"Your name was familiar to me long before I knew you personally. I had often heard of 'Professor W. G. Allen,' who, while connected with the Central College, in the State of New York, and respected there as a man and a teacher, was obliged to leave his native country for the offence of marrying a white lady of respectable family and great excellence of character, who is now much liked and esteemed by her numerous friends in this city.

I became acquainted with you soon after your arrival in London; and particularly during your residence in Ireland I have had nearly as much opportunity of knowing you as any of your acquaintances here. I can truly say, that you have earned the hearty respect of all who know you (of whom I have any knowledge), by the industry, energy, and self-respect you have evinced in the course of a long and difficult battle with those adverse circumstances, with which a comparatively unknown and friendless stranger has to contend, in his efforts to effect a settlement in a strange country. Your conduct has been industrious, honorable and in every way deserving of esteem and sympathy. Some time since, in the columns of the 'Anti-Slavery Advocate,' without hint or solicitation on your part, I took the liberty to speak of your course as I do now; for amongst all the colored Americans with whom my interest in the Anti-Slavery cause has made me acquainted—and many of whom are my own personal friends—I have known none more deserving of respect and confidence than yourself.

"Yours truly,

"RICHARD, D. WEBB."

HAVING, in my avocation as lecturer on "The African Race" and "America and the Americans," visited nearly the whole of Ireland, I respectfully submit the following letters and notices, the letters being from gentlemen who kindly presided at the meetings:—

From the Rev. DOCTOR FITZGERALD, Archdeacon of Kildare, (now Lord Bishop of Cork).

"Professor Allen delivered some lectures on the African Race, in Kingstown, which seemed to have given general satisfaction. I regret that I was unable to attend more than one, but I can truly say that it bore evidence of a highly cultivated mind, and imparted valuable information in a pleasing form. From what I have seen and heard of Professor Allen, I should be glad to think that any testimony of mine could be of service to him.

"W. FITZGERALD, Archdeacon of Kildare,
(Now Lord Bishop of Cork.)
"Dublin, Nov. 1856"

From Rev. DOCTOR URWICK, Dublin.

"I have known Professor Allen since his first coming to Ireland, and believe him to be a gentleman of high character and attainments. His lecturings, more than one of which I have heard, display much power, and by the amount of information they contain, united with a clear and often eloquent style, and earnest manner, cannot fail, at once, to interest and instruct the audience. I cordially commend him to the confidence and kind attention of my friends.

"W. URWICK.
"Dublin, Nov. 30, 1857."

From CORK—see "Constitution," "Examiner" and
"Reporter," March 1858.

"Cork, Feb. 28, 1858.
"To WILLIAM G. ALLEN, Esq. late Professor of Greek in
New York Central College.

"DEAR SIR—We, the undersigned, having heard your lectures on 'America' and 'Africa,' and derived therefrom much instruction as well as gratification, do, on our own part and that of many of our fellow citizens who are anxious to hear you, respectfully request that you will give, at least, two lectures more upon these interesting subjects.

"(Signed)
HENRY MARTIN, Congregational Minister.
R. W. FORREST (Free Church).
RICHD. CORBETT, M. D.

J. D. CARNEGIE.
HENRY UNKLES.
GEORGE BAKER.
RICHARD DOWDEN, (Rd.)
WILLIAM MAGILL, (Scots' Church).
JOSEPH R. GREENE, Professor, Queen's Coll.
THOMAS JENNINGS.
N. JACKSON, C. E.
JOSEPH COLBECK."

From "Belfast News-letter," Dec. 10, 1858.

"REV. DOCTOR COOKE occupied the chair. Professor Allen then delivered a lecture of great ability and interest. Dr. Cooke said he had listened to a remarkable oration. He was glad he had heard it. He thanked Professor Allen, in the name of the meeting, for his truly valuable and instructive lecture."

From the DEAN OF WATERFORD.

"Professor W. G. Allen, an American gentleman of color, having visited Waterford, delivered two lectures here, one on 'America,' and the other on 'Africa and the African Races.' On each occasion I had the pleasure to occupy the chair at the meetings held to hear Mr. Allen's lectures, which proved most interesting and instructive. The Professor is himself a witness that there is nothing in color or race to hinder a man from being distinguished for eloquence, good taste, and religious feeling.

"I have seldom heard public addresses which have interested me more, and I have no doubt that Mr. Allen's lectures will prove useful, wherever they are delivered, in creating an interest on behalf of our fellow men, who have suffered so great wrongs from professing Christians, though happily no longer at the hands of British subjects.

"EDW. N. HOARE,
Dean of Waterford.

"Deanery, Waterford, Jan. 16, 1858."

From Rev. DOCTOR BROWNE, Principal of Kilkenny College.

"Kilkenny College, Feb. 3, 1858.

"I have attended Professor Allen's lectures on 'America and the Americans,' and on the 'African Races,' and have received much pleasure as well as information from the talent and power with which he has handled the subjects of which he treated.

"His knowledge, his ardent and impressive manner, and clear melodious voice, render him a most pleasing as well as instructive lecturer.

"JOHN BROWNE, Clk. LL.D."

M.L.

BY LOUISA MAY ALCOTT

M.L.

CHAPTER I

He spoke, and words more soft than rain
The sun set—but not his hope:
Stars rose—his face was earlier up:
He spoke, and words more soft than rain
Brought back the Age of Gold again:
His action won such reverence sweet,
As hid all measure of the feat.

HUSH! let me listen."

Mrs. Snowden ceased her lively gossip, obedient to the command, and leaning her head upon her hand, Claudia sat silent.

Like a breath of purer air, the music floated through the room, bringing an exquisite delight to the gifted few, and stirring the dullest nature with a sense of something nobler than it knew. Frivolous women listened mutely, pleasure-seeking men confessed its charm, world-worn spirits lived again the better moments of their lives, and wounded hearts found in it a brief solace for the griefs so jealously concealed. At its magic touch the masks fell from many faces and a momentary softness made them fair, eye met eye with rare sincerity, false smiles faded, vapid conversation died abashed, and for a little space, Music, the divine enchantress, asserted her supremacy, wooing tenderly as any woman, ruling royally as any queen.

Like water in a desert place, Claudia's thirsty spirit drank in the silver sounds that fed her ear, and through the hush they came to her like a remembered strain. Their varying power swayed her like a wizard's wand, its subtle softness wrapped her senses in a blissful calm, its passion thrilled along her nerves like south winds full of an aroma fiery and sweet, its energy stirred her blood like martial music or heroic speech,—for this mellow voice seemed to bring her the low sigh of pines, the ardent breath of human lips, the grand anthem of the sea. It held her fast, and lifting her above the narrow bounds of time and place, blessed her with a loftier mood than she had ever known before, for midsummer night and warmth seemed born of it, and her solitary nature yearned to greet the genial influence as frost-bound grasses spring to meet the sun.

What the song was, she never heard, she never cared to know; to other ears it might be love-lay, barcarole, or miserere for the dead,—to her it was a melody devout and sweet as saintliest hymn, for it had touched the chords of that diviner self whose aspirations are the flowers of life, it had soothed the secret pain of a proud spirit, it had stirred the waters of a lonely heart, and from their depths a new born patience rose with healing on its wings.

Silent she sat, one hand above her eyes, the other lying in her lap, unmoved since with her last words it rose and fell. The singer had been forgotten in the song, but as the music with triumphant swell soared upward and grew still, the spell was broken, the tide of conversation flowed again, and with an impatient sigh, Claudia looked up and saw her happy dream depart.

"Who is this man? you told me but I did not hear."

With the eagerness of a born gossip, Mrs. Snowden whispered the tale a second time in her friend's ear.

"This man (as you would never call him had you seen him) is a Spaniard, and of noble family, I'm sure, though he denies it. He is poor, of course,—these interesting exiles always are,— he teaches music, and though an accomplished gentleman and as proud as if the 'blue blood' of all the grandees of Spain flowed in his veins, he will not own to any rank, but steadily asserts that he is 'plain Paul Frere, trying honestly to earn his bread, and nothing more.' Ah, you like that, and the very thing that disappoints me most, will make the man a hero in your eyes."

"Honesty is an heroic virtue, and I honor it wherever it is found. What further, Jessie?" and Claudia looked a shade more interested than when the chat began.

"Only that in addition to his charming voice, he is a handsome soul, beside whom our pale-faced gentlemen look boyish and insipid to a mortifying degree. Endless romances are in progress, of which he may be the hero if he will, but unfortunately for his fair pupils the fine eyes of their master seem blind to any 'tremolo movements' but those set down in the book; and he hears them warble *'O mio Fernando'* in the tenderest of spoken languages as tranquilly as if it were a nursery song. He leads a solitary life, devoted to his books and art, and rarely mixes in the society of which *I* think him a great ornament. This is all I know concerning him, and if you ever care to descend from your Mont Blanc of cool indifference, I fancy this minstrel will pay you for the effort. Look! that is he, the dark man with the melancholy eyes; deign to give me your opinion of my modern 'Thaddeus.' "

Claudia looked well, and, as she did so, vividly before her mind's eye rose a picture she had often pondered over when a child.

A painting of a tropical island, beautiful with the bloom and verdure of the South. An ardent sky, flushed with sunrise canopied the scene, palm trees lifted their crowned heads far into the fervid air, orange groves dropped dark shadows on the sward where flowers in rank luxuriance glowed like spires of flame, or shone like stars among the green. Bright-hued birds swung on vine and bough, dainty gazelles lifted their human eyes to greet the sun, and a summer sea seemed to flow low— singing to the bloomy shore. The first blush and dewiness of dawn lay over the still spot, but looking nearer, the eye saw that the palm's green crowns were rent, the vines hung torn as if by ruthless gusts, and the orange boughs were robbed of half their wealth, for fruit and flowers lay thick upon the sodden earth. Far on the horizon's edge, a thunderous cloud seemed rolling westward, and on the waves an ominous wreck swayed with the swaying of the treacherous sea.

Claudia saw a face that satisfied her eye as the voice had done her ear, and yet its comeliness was not its charm. Black locks streaked an ample forehead, black brows arched finely over southern eyes as full of softness as of fire. No color marred the pale bronze of the cheek, no beard hid the firm contour of the lips, no unmeaning smile destroyed the dignity of a thoughtful countenance, on which nature's hand had set the seal wherewith she stamps the manhood that no art can counterfeit.

But as she searched it deeper, Claudia saw upon the forehead lines that seldom come to men of thirty, in the eye the shadow of some past despair, and about the closely folded lips traces of an impetuous nature tamed by suffering and taught by time. Here, as in the picture, the tempest seemed to have gone by, but though a gracious day had come, the cloud had left a shade behind. Sweet winds came wooingly from off the shore, and the sea serenely smiled above the wreck, but a vague unrest still stirred the air, and an undertone of human woe still whispered through the surges' song.

"So Dante might have looked before his genius changed the crown of thorns into a crown of roses for the woman he loved," thought Claudia, then said aloud in answer to her friend's last words,

"Yes, I like that face, less for its beauty than its strength. I like that austere simplicity of dress, that fine unconsciousness of self, and more than all I like the courtesy with which he listens to the poorest, plainest, least attractive woman in the room. Laugh, if you will, Jessie, I respect him more for his kindness to neglected Mary Low, than if for a fairer woman he had fought as many battles as Saint George. This is true courtesy, and it is the want of this reverence for womanhood in itself, which makes many of our so-called gentlemen what they are, and robs them of one attribute of real manliness."

"Heaven defend us! here is an Alpine avalanche of praise from our Diana! Come, be made known to this Endymion before you can congeal again," cried Jessie; for Claudia's words were full of energy, and in her eye shone an interest that softened its cold brilliancy and gave her countenance the warmth which was the charm it needed most. Claudia went, and soon found herself enjoying the delights of conversation in the finer sense of that word. Paul Frere did not offer her the stale compliments men usually think it proper to bestow upon a woman, as if her mind were like a dainty purse too limited for any small coin of any worth, nor did he offer her the witty gossips current in society, which, like crisp bank bills, rustle pleasantly, and are accepted as a "counterfeit presentiment," of that silver speech, which should marry sound to sense. He gave her sterling gold, that rang true to the ear, and bore the stamp of genuine belief, for unconsciously he put himself into his words, and made them what they should be,—the interpreters of one frank nature to another.

He took the few pale phantoms custom has condemned to serve as subjects of discourse between a man and a woman in a place like that, and giving them vitality and color, they became the actors of his thought, and made a living drama of that little hour. Yet he was no scholar erudite and polished by long study or generous culture. Adversity had been his college, experience his tutor, and life the book whose lessons stern and salutary he had learned with patient pain. Real wrong and suffering and want had given him a knowledge no philosopher could teach, real danger and desolation had lifted him above the petty fears that take the heroism out of daily life, and a fiery baptism had consecrated heart and mind and soul to one great aim, beside which other men's ambitions seemed most poor. This was the secret charm he owned, this gave the simplicity that dignified his manner, the sincerity that won in his address; this proved the supremacy of character over culture, opulence and rank, and made him what he was—a man to command respect and confidence and love.

Dimly Claudia saw, and vaguely felt all this in that brief interview; but when it ended, she wished it were to come again, and felt as if she had left the glare and glitter of the stage whereon she played her part, for a moment had put off her mask to sit down in the ruddy circle of a household fire where little shadows danced upon the walls, and tender tones made common speech divine.

"It will be gone tomorrow, this pleasure beautiful and brief, and I shall fall back into my old disappointment again, as I have always done before"; she sighed within herself. Yet when she sat alone in her own home, it seemed no longer solitary, and like a happy child she lulled herself to sleep with fitful snatches of a song she had never heard but once.

CHAPTER II

CLAUDIA stood alone in the world, a woman of strong character and independent will, gifted with beauty, opulence and position, possessing the admiration and esteem of many, the affection of a few whose love was worth desiring. All these good gifts were hers, and yet she was not satisfied. Home ties she had never known, mother-love had only blessed her long enough to make its loss most keenly felt, the sweet confidence of sisterhood had never warmed her with its innocent delights, "father" and "brother" were unknown words upon her lips, for she had never known the beauty and the strength of man's most sincere affection.

Many hands had knocked at the closed door, but knocked in vain, for the master had not come, and true to her finer instincts, Claudia would not make a worldly marriage or try to cheat her hunger into a painted feast. She would have all or nothing, and when friends urged or lovers pleaded, she answered steadily:

"I cannot act a lie, and receive where I have nothing to bestow. If I am to know the blessedness of love, it will come to me, and I can wait."

Love repaid her loyalty at last. Through the close-scented air of the conservatory where she had lived a solitary plant, there came a new influence, like a breath of ocean air, both strengthening and sweet. Then the past ceased to be a mournful memory; for over her lost hopes, the morning glories that had early died,—over her eager desires, the roses that had never bloomed—over broken friendships, the nests whence all the birds were flown—a pleasant twilight seemed to fall, and across the sombre present came the ruddy herald of a future dawn. It brought the magic moment when the flower could bloom, the master's hand whose touch unbarred the door, the charmed voice that woke the sleeping princess, and sang to her of

"That new world, which is the old".

In "plain Paul Frere," Claudia found her hero, recognized her king, although like Bruce he came in minstrel guise and accepted royally the alms bestowed.

Slowly, by rare interviews, the swift language of the eye, and music's many wiles, Paul caught deeper glimpses into Claudia's solitary life, and felt the charm of an earnest nature shining through the maidenly reserve that veiled it from his search. He sang to her, and singing, watched the still fire that kindled in her eye, the content that touched her lips with something softer than a smile, the warmth that stole so beautifully to her face, melting the pride that chilled it, banishing the weariness that saddened it, and filling it with light, and hope, and bloom, as if at his command the woman's sorrows fell away and left a happy girl again. It was a dangerous power to wield, but with the consciousness of its possession came a sentiment that curbed a strong man's love of power, and left the subject to a just man's love of right.

He denied himself the happiness of ministering to Claudia the frequent feasts she loved, for it was offering her a wine more subtle than she knew, a wine whose potency her friend already felt. He seldom sang to her alone, but conversation was a rich reward for this renunciation, for in those hours, beautiful and brief, he found an interest that "grew by what it fed on," and soon felt that it was fast becoming sweeter to receive than to bestow.

Claudia was a student of like dangerous lore, for she too scanned her new friend warily and well; often with keen perceptions divining what she dared not seek, with swift instincts feeling what she could not see. Her first judgments had been just, her first impressions never changed. For each month of increasing friendship, was one of increasing honor and esteem.

This man who earned his bread, and asked no favors where he might have demanded many, who would accept no fictitious rank, listen to no flattering romance, who bore the traces of a fateful past, yet showed no bitterness of spirit, but went his way steadfastly, living to some high end unseen by human eyes, yet all-sustaining in itself,—this man seemed to Claudia the friend she had desired, for here she found a character built up by suffering and time, an eager intellect aspiring for the true, and valiant spirit looking straight and strong into the world.

To her ear the music of his life became more beautiful than any lay he sang, and on his shield her heart inscribed the fine old lines,

> "Lord of himself, though not of lands,
> And having nothing, yet hath all."

CHAPTER III

ONE balmy night, when early flowers were blossoming in Claudia's garden, and the west wind was the almoner of their sweet charities, she sat looking with thoughtful eyes into the shadowy stillness of the hour.

Miss Blank, the mild nonentity who played propriety in Claudia's house, had been absorbed into the darkness of an inner room, where sleep might descend upon her weary eyelids without an open breach of that decorum which was the good soul's staff of life.

Paul Frere, leaning in the shadow, looked down upon the bent head whereon the May moon dropped a shining benediction; and as he looked, his countenance grew young again with hope, and fervent with strong desire. Silence had fallen on them, for watching *her*, Paul forgot to speak, and Claudia was plucking leaf after leaf from a flower that had strayed from among the knot that graced her breast. One by one the crimson petals fluttered to the ground, and as she saw them fall a melancholy shadow swept across her face.

"What has the rose done that its life should be so short?" her friend asked as the last leaf left her hand.

As if the words recalled her to the present, Claudia looked at the dismantled stem, saying regretfully, "I forgot the flower, and now I have destroyed it with no skill to make it live again." She paused a moment, then added smiling as if at her own fancies, though the regretful cadence lingered in her voice, "This is my birth-night, and thinking of my past, the rose ceased to be a rose to me, and became a little symbol of my life. Each leaf I gathered seemed a year, and as it fell I thought how fast, how vainly, they had gone. They should have been fairer in aspirations, fuller of duties, richer in good deeds, happier in those hopes that make existence sweet, but now it is too late. Poor rose! Poor life!" and from the smiling lips there fell a sigh.

Paul took the relic of the rose, and with a gesture soft as a caress, broke from the stem a little bud just springing from its mossy sheath, saying with a glance as full of cheer as hers had been of despondency, "My friend, it never is too late. Out of the loneliest life may bloom a higher beauty than the lost rose knew. Let the first sanguine petals fall, their perfume will remain a pleasant memory when they are dead; but cherish the fairer flower that comes so late, nurture it with sunshine, baptise it with dew, and though the garden never knows it more, it may make summer in some shady spot and bless a household with its breath and bloom. I have no gift wherewith to celebrate this night, but let me give you back a happier emblem of the life to be, and with it a prophecy that when another six and twenty years are gone, no sigh will mar your smile as you look back and say, 'Fair rose! Fair life!'"

Claudia looked up with traitorous eyes, and answered softly—"I accept the prophecy, and will fulfil it, if the black frost does not fall." Then with a wistful glance and all persuasive tone, she added, "You have forgotten one gift always in your power to bestow. Give it to me to-night, and usher in my happier years with music."

There was no denial to a request like that, and with a keen sense of delight Paul obeyed, singing as he had never sung before, for heart and soul were in the act, and all benignant influences lent their aid to beautify his gift. The silence of the night received the melody, and sent it whispering back like ripples breaking on the shore; the moonbeams danced like elves upon the keys, as if endowing human touch with their magnetic power; the west wind tuned its leafy orchestra to an airy symphony, and every odorous shrub and flower paid tribute to the happy hour.

With drooping lids and lips apart, Claudia listened, till on the surges of sweet sound her spirit floated far away into that blissful realm where human aspirations are fulfilled, where human hearts find their ideals, and renew again the innocent beliefs that made their childhood green.

Silence fell suddenly, startling Claudia from her dream. For a moment the radiance of the room grew dark before her eyes, then a swift light dawned, and in it she beheld the countenance of her friend transfigured by the power of that great passion which heaven has gifted with eternal youth. For a long moment nothing stirred, and across the little space that parted them the two regarded one another with wordless lips, but eyes whose finer language made all speech impertinent.

Paul bent on the woman whom he loved a look more tender than the most impassioned prayer, more potent than the subtlest appeal, more eloquent than the most fervent vow. He saw the maiden color flush and fade, saw the breath quicken and the lips grow tremulous, but the steadfast eyes never wavered, never fell, and through those windows of the soul, her woman's heart looked out and answered him.

There was no longer any doubt or fear or power to part them now, and with a gesture full of something nobler than Pride, Paul stretched his hand to Claudia, and she took it fast in both her own.

To a believer in metempsychosis it would have been an easy task to decide the last shape Mrs. Snowden had endowed with life, for the old fable of the "cat transformed into a woman," might have been again suggested to a modern Aesop.

Soft of manner, smooth of tongue, stealthy of eye, this feline lady followed out the instincts of her nature with the fidelity of any veritable puss. With demure aspect and pleasant purrings she secured the admiration of innocents who forgot that velvet paws could scratch, and the friendship of comfortable souls who love to pet and be amused. Daintily picking her way through the troubles of this life, she slipped into cosy corners where rugs were softest and fires warmest, gambolling delightfully while the cream was plentiful, and the caresses graciously bestowed. Gossips and scandal were the rats and mice she feasted on, the prey she paraded with ill-disguised exultation when her prowlings and pouncings had brought them to light. Many a smart robin had been fascinated by her power, or escaping left his plumes behind; many a meek mouse had implored mercy for its indiscretion but found none, and many a blithe cricket's music ended when she glided through the grass. Dark holes and corners were hunted by her keen eye, the dust of forgotten rumors was disturbed by her covert tread, and secrets were hunted out with most untiring patience.

She had her enemies, what puss has not? Sundry honest mastiffs growled when she entered their domains, but scorned to molest a weaker foe; sundry pugs barked valiantly till she turned on them and with un-sheathed claws administered a swift quietus to their wrath; sundry jovial squirrels cracked their jokes and flourished defiance, but skipped nimbly from her way, and chattered on a bow she could not climb. More than one friend had found the pantry pillaged, and the milk of human kindness lapped dry by an indefatigable tongue; and yet no meeker countenance lifted its pensive eyes in church, no voice more indignantly rebuked the shortcomings of her race, and no greater martyr bewailed ingratitude when doors were shut upon her, and stern housewives shouted "scat!"

Wifehood and widowhood had only increased her love of freedom and confirmed her love of power. Claudia pitied her, and when others blamed, defended or excused, for her generous nature had no knowledge of duplicity or littleness of soul. Jessie seemed all candor, and though superficial, was full of winning ways and tender confidences that seemed sincere, and very pleasant to the other's lonely heart. So Jessie haunted her friend's house, rode triumphantly in her carriage, made a shield of her regard, and disported herself at her expense, till a stronger force appeared, and the widow's reign abruptly ended.

The May moon had shown on Claudia's betrothal, and the harvest moon would shine upon her marriage. The months passed like a happy dream, and the midsummer of her life was in its prime. The stir and tattle that went on about her was like an idle wind, for she had gone out of the common world and believed that she cared little for its censure or its praise. What mattered it that Paul was poor—she was not rich? What mattered it that she knew little of his past—had she not all the present and the future for her own? What cared she for the tongues that called him "fortune-hunter," and herself romantic? he possessed a better fortune than any she could give, and she was blessed with a romance that taught her wiser lessons than reality had ever done. So they went their way, undisturbed by any wind that blew. Paul still gave her lessons, still retained his humble home as if no change had befallen him, and Claudia with all her energies alert, bestirred herself to "set her house in order, and make ready for the bridegroom's coming." But as each night fell, patient Teacher, busy Housewife vanished, and two lovers met. The sun set on all their cares, and twilight shed a peace upon them softer than the dew, for Joy was the musician now, and Love the fairy hostess of the guests who made high festival of that still hour.

The months had dwindled to a week, and in the gloaming of a sultry day, Paul came early to his tryst. Claudia was detained by lingering guests, and with a frown at their delay, her lover paced the room until she should come. Pausing suddenly in his restless march, Paul drew a letter from his breast and read it slowly as if his thoughts had been busy with its contents. It was a letter of many pages, written in decided characters, worn as if with frequent reading, and as he turned it his face wore a look it had never shown to Claudia's eyes. With a sudden impulse he raised his right hand to the light, and scanned it with a strange scrutiny. Across the palm stretched a wide purple scar, the relic of some wound healed long ago, but not effaced by time. Claudia had once asked as she caressed it what blow had left so deep a trace, and he had answered with a sudden clenching of the hand, a sudden fire in the eye, "Claudia, it is the memorial of a victory I won ten years ago; it was a righteous battle, but its memory is bitter. Let it sleep; and believe me, it is an honest hand, or I could never look in your true face and give it you again."

She had been content, and never touched the sad past by a word, for she wholly trusted where she wholly loved.

As Paul looked thoughtfully at that right hand of his, the left dropped at his side, and from among the loosely held papers, a single sheet escaped, and fluttered noiselessly among the white folds of the draperies, that swept the floor. The stir of departing feet aroused him from his reverie; with a quick gesture he crushed the letter, and lit it at the Roman lamp that always burned for him. Slowly the fateful pages shrivelled and grew black; silently he watched them burn, and when the last flame flickered and went out, he gathered up the ashes and gave them to the keeping of the wind. Then all the shadows faded from his face, and left the old composure there.

Claudia's voice called from below, and with the ardor of a boy he sprang down to meet the welcome he was hungering for.

As the door closed behind him, from the gloom of that inner room Jessie Snowden stole out and seized her prize. Listening with sharpened sense for any coming step, she swept the page with her keen eye, gathering its meaning before a dozen lines were read. The paper rustled with the tremor of her hand, and for a moment the room spun dizzily before her as she dropped into a seat, and sat staring straight into the air with a countenance where exultation and bewilderment were strangely blended. "Poor Claudia," was the first thought that took shape in her mind, but a harder one usurped its place, an ominous glitter shone in her black eyes, as she muttered with a wicked smile, "I owe him this, and he shall have it."

An hour later Paul and Claudia sat in that same spot together, not yet content, for opposite still lounged Jessie Snowden, showing no symptoms of departure. Her cheek burned with a brilliant color, her black eyes glittered with repressed excitement and in gesture, look and tone there was a peculiar sharpness as if every sense were unwontedly alert, every nerve unwontedly high strung. She was not loquacious, but seemed waiting till speech would take effect; for all her feline instincts were awake, and she must torture a little before she dealt the blow. She knew the lovers wished her gone, yet still sat watchful and wary, till the auspicious moment came.

Paul was restless, for his southern temperament, more keenly alive to subtle influences than colder natures, vaguely warned him of the coming blow, unwillingly yielded to the baleful power it could not comprehend, unconsciously betrayed that Jessie's presence brought disquiet, and so doing placed a weapon in her hand, which she did not fail to use. Her eye was on him constantly, with a glance that stirred him like an insult, while it held him like a spell. His courtesy was sorely tried, for whether he spoke or was mute, moved about the room or sat with averted face, he felt that eye still on him, with a look of mingled hatred, pity and contempt. He confronted it and bore it down; but when he turned, it rose again and haunted him with its aggressive shine. He fixed his regard on Claudia, and so forgot for a time, but it was always there and proved itself no fancy of a tired brain.

Claudia was weary and grudged the quiet hour which always left her refreshed, when no unwelcome presence marred its charm. She was unutterably tired of Jessie, and if a wish could have secured her absence, she would have vanished with the speed of a stage sprite at the wizard's will.

"Is't the old pain, Paul? Let me play Desdemona, and bind my handkerchief about your forehead as I have done before," and Claudia's voice soothed the ear with unspoken love.

Paul had leaned his head upon his hand, but as she spoke he lifted it and answered cheerfully, "I have no pain, but something in the atmosphere oppresses me. I fancy there is thunder in the air."

"There is"—and Jessie laughed a laugh that had no mirth in it, as she sat erect with sudden interest in her voice.

Paul swept aside the curtain, and looked out; the sky was cloudless and the evening star hung luminous and large on the horizon's edge.

"Ah, you think I am a false prophet, but wait an hour then look again. *I* see a fierce storm rolling up, though the cloud is 'no bigger than a man's hand' now."

As she spoke Jessie's eye glanced across the hand Paul had extended for the fan which Claudia was offering; he did not see the look, but unfurling the daintily carved toy, answered calmly as the stirred air cooled the fever of his cheek: "I cannot doubt you, Mrs. Snowden, for you look truly sibylline tonight; but if you read the future with such a gifted eye, can you not find us a fairer future than your storm foretells?"

"Did you ever know before that there was gipsy blood in my veins, and that I possessed the gipsy's power of second sight? Shall I use it, and tell your fortune like a veritable witch? May I, Claudia?"

Jessie's friend looked at her with a touch of wonder; for the flush was deepening on her cheek, the fire kindling in her eyes, and her whole aspect seemed to stir and brighten like a snake's before it springs.

"If Paul pleases I should like to hear your 'rede,' and we will cross your palm with silver by and by. Indeed I think the inspired phrenzy is descending upon you, Jessie, for you look like an electric battery fully charged, and I dare not touch you lest I should receive a shock," Claudia answered, smiling at the sudden change.

"I *am* a battery to-night, and you *may* have your shock whenever you please. Come, Mr. Frere, your sovereign consents, come and let me try my power—if you dare."

A slight frown contracted Paul's brows, and a disdainful smile flitted across his lips; but Claudia waited and he silently obeyed.

"Not this hand, fate lies only in the *right*."

"Jessie, take mine instead, our fortunes henceforth will be the same!" cried Claudia, with eager voice remembering the mark Paul never showed.

But Jessie only laughed the metallic laugh again, clear and sharp as the jangle of a bell; and with a gesture of something like defiance Paul stretched his right hand to her, while the disdainful smile still sat upon his lips. Jessie did not touch it, but bent and scanned it eagerly, though nothing could be seen but the wide scar across the shapely palm.

A dead silence fell upon the three. Paul stood composed and motionless, Jessie paled visibly, and the quick throb of her heart grew audible, but Claudia felt the pain of that rude scrutiny, and leaning toward them asked impatiently, "Sibyl, what do you read?"

Jessie swayed slowly backward, and looking up at the defiant face above her, answered in a whisper that cut the silence like a knife.

"I see two letters,—M. L."

Paul did not start, his countenance did not change, but the fan dropped shattered from his grasp—the only sign that he had heard. Claudia's eyes were on them, but she could not speak, and the sibilant whisper came again.

"I know it all, for *this* remained to tell the secret, and *I* am the master now. See here!" and with a peal of laughter Jessie threw the paper at his feet.

CHAPTER IV

PAUL gave one glance at the crumpled sheet, then turned on her with a look that sent her trembling to the door, as a gust would sweep a thistle down before it. It was the look of a hunted creature, driven to bay; wrath, abhorrence, and despair stirred the strong man's frame, looked out at his desperate eye, strengthened his uplifted arm, and had not his opponent been a woman some swift retribution would have fallen on her, for there was murder in his fiery blood.

Claudia sprang to his side, and at the touch of those restraining hands a stern pallor settled on his countenance, a hard-won self-control quenched his passion, a bitter truth confronted his despair, and left him desolate but not degraded. His eye fixed on Jessie, and its hopelessness was more eloquent than a torrent of entreaties, its contempt more keen than the sharpest reproach.

"Go," he said with a strange hush in his voice, "I ask nothing of you, for I know you would be merciless to me; but if there be any compassion, any touch of nobleness in your nature you will spare your friend, remembering what she has been to you. Go, and mar my hard-won reputation as you will, the world's condemnation I will not accept, my judge is *here*."

"There will be no need of silence a week hence when the marriage day comes around and there is no bridegroom for the bride. I foretold the storm, and it has come; heaven help you through it, Claudia. Good night, pleasant dreams, and a fair tomorrow!"

Jessie Snowden tried to look exultant, but her white lips would not smile, and though the victory was hers she crept away like one who has suffered defeat.

Paul locked the door behind her, and turning, looked at Claudia with a world of anguish in his altered face. She moved as if to go to him, but a gesture arrested her, and uttering a broken exclamation Paul struck his scarred hand on the chimney piece with a force that left it bruised and bleeding, and dropping his hot forehead on the marble stood silent, struggling with a grief that had no solace.

Claudia paused a moment, mute and pale, watching the bowed figure and the red drops as they fell, then she went to him, and holding the wounded palm as if it were a suffering child, she laid her cheek to his, whispering tenderly: "Paul, you said this was an honest hand and I believe it still. There should not be a grain of dust between us two,—deal frankly with me now, and let me comfort you."

Paul lifted up his face wan with the tearless sorrow of a man, and gathering the beloved comforter close to his sore heart looked long into the countenance whose loving confidence had no reproach for him as yet. He held her fast for a little space, kissed her lips and forehead lingeringly, as if he took a mute farewell, then gently put her from him saying, as she sank into a seat—

"Claudia, I never meant to burden you with my unhappy past, believing that I did no wrong in burying it deep from human sight, and walking through the world as if it had never been. I see my error now, and bitterly I repent it. Put pity, prejudice, and pride away, and see me as I am. Hear and judge me, and by your judgment I will abide."

He paused, silently gathering calmness from his strength, and courage from his love; then, as if each word were wrung from him by a sharper pang than he had ever known before, he said slowly: "Claudia, those letters were once branded on my hand, they are the initials of a name—'Maurice Lecroix.' Ten years ago he was my master, I his slave."

If Paul had raised his strong right arm and struck her, the act would not have daunted her with such a pale dismay, or shocked the power more rudely from her limbs. For an instant the tall shape wavered mistily before her and her heart stood still; then she girded up her energies, for with her own suffering came the memory of his, and, true woman through it all, she only covered up her face and cried: "Go on, I can hear it, Paul!"

Solemnly and steadily, as if it were his dying shrift, Paul stood before the woman he loved and told the story of his life.

"My father—God forgive him—was a Cuban planter, my mother a beautiful Quadroon, mercifully taken early out of slavery to an eternal freedom. I never knew her but she bequeathed to me my father's love, and I possessed it till he died. For fifteen years I was a happy child, and forgot that I was a slave—light tasks, kind treatment, and slight restraints so blinded me to the real hardships of my lot. I had a sister, heiress of my father's name and fortune, and she was my playmate all those years, sharing her pleasures and her pains with me, her small store of knowledge, her girlish accomplishments as she acquired them, and—more than all—the blessing of an artless love. I was her proud protector, her willing servitor, and in those childish days we were what heaven made us, brother and sister fond and free.

"I was fifteen when my father died, and the black blight fell upon me in a single night. He had often promised me my freedom—strange gift from a father to a son!—but like other duties it had been neglected till too late. Death came suddenly, and I was left a sadder orphan than poor Nathalie, for my heritage was a curse that cancelled all past love by robbing me of liberty.

"Nathalie and I were separated—she went to her guardian's protection, I to the auction block. Her last words were, 'Be kind to Paul.' They promised; but when she was gone they sold me far away from my old home, and then I learned what it was to be a slave. Ah, Claudia, you shudder when I say those words; give your abhorrence to the man who dared to love you, but bestow a little pity on the desolate boy you never knew. I had a hard master, he a rebellious spirit to subdue; for I could not learn subjection, and my young blood burned within me at an insult or a blow. My father's kindness proved the direst misfortune that could have befallen me, for I had been lifted up into humanity and now I was cast back among the brutes; I had been born with a high heart and an eager spirit, they had been cherished fifteen years, now they were to be crushed and broken by inevitable fate.

"Year after year I struggled on, growing more desperate, and tugging more fiercely at my chain as each went by, bringing manhood but not the right to enjoy or make it mine. I tried to escape, but in vain, and each failure added to my despair. I tried to hear of Nathalie, but she had learned to look on me in another light, and had forgotten the sweet tie that bound us once. I tried to become a chattel and be content, but my father had given me his own free instincts, aspirations, and desires, and I could not change my nature though I were to be a slave forever.

"Five miserable years dragged by—so short to tell of, such an eternity to live! I was twenty, and no young man ever looked into the world more eager to be up and doing, no young man ever saw so black a future as that which appalled me with its doom. I would not accept it, but made a last resolve to try once more for liberty, and if I failed, to end the life I could no longer bear. Watchfully I waited, warily I planned, desperately I staked my last hope—and lost it. I was betrayed and hunted down as ruthlessly as any wolf; but I tried to keep my vow; for as my pursuers clutched me I struck the blow that should have ended all, and the happiest moment of my life was that swift pang when the world passed from me with the exultant thought, 'I am free at last!'"

Paul paused, spent and breathless with rapid speech and strong emotion, and in the silence heard Claudia murmuring through a rain of tears: "Oh, my love! my love! was there no friend but death?"

That low cry was a stronger cordial to Paul's spirit than the rarest wine grape that ever grew. He looked yearningly across the narrow space that parted them, but though his eye blessed her for her pity, he did not pass the invisible barrier he had set up between them till her hand should throw it down or fix it there forever.

"These are bitter things for you to hear, dear heart. God knows they were bitter things to bear, but I am stronger for them now and you the calmer for your tears. A little more and happier times are coming. I could not lie, but came out of that 'valley of the shadow' a meeker soul; for though branded, buffeted, and bruised, I clung to life, blindly believing help must come, and it did. One day a shape passed before my eyes that seemed the angel of deliverance—it was Nathalie, and she was my master's guest. I gathered covertly that she was a gentle-woman, that she was mistress of her fortune now, and soon to be a happy wife; and hearing these things I determined to make one appeal to her in my great need.

"I watched her, and one blessed night, defying every penalty, and waiting till the house was still, and her light burned alone as I had seen it many times before, I climbed the balcony and stood before her saying, 'I am Paul, help me in our father's name.' She did not recognize the blithe boy in the desperate man, but I told my misery, implored compassion and relief, I looked at her with her father's face, and nature pleaded better than my prayers, for she stretched her hands to me, saying, with tears as beautiful as those now shining on your cheek, 'Who should help you if not I? Be comforted and I will atone for this great neglect and wrong. Paul, have faith in me; I shall not fail.'

"Claudia, you loved me first for my great reverence for woman-kind; this is the secret of the virtue you commend, for when I was most desolate a woman succored me. Since then, in every little maid, I see the child who loved me when a boy, in every blooming girl, the Nathalie who saved me when a man, in every woman, high or low, the semblance of my truest friend, and do them honor in my sister's name."

"Heaven crown her with a happy life!" prayed Claudia, with fervent heart, and still more steadily her lover's voice went on.

"She kept her word, and did a just deed generously, for money flowed like water till I was free, then giving me a little store for present needs, she sent me out the richest man that walked the world. I left the island and went to and fro seeking for my place upon the earth. I never told my story, never betrayed my past, I have no sign of my despised race but my Spanish hue, and taking my father's native country for my own I found no bar in swarthy skin, or the only name I had a right to bear. I seared away all traces of a master's claim, and smiled as the flame tortured me, for liberty had set her seal upon my forehead, and my flesh and blood were *mine*.

"Then I took the rights and duties of a man upon me, feeling their weight and worth, looking proudly on them as a sacred trust won by much suffering, to be used worthily and restored to their bestower richer for my stewardship. I looked about me for some work to do, for now I labored for myself, and industry was sweet. I was a stranger in a strange land, friendless and poor; but I had energy and hope, two angels walking with me night and day.

"Music had always been my passion; now I chose it as my staff of life. In hospitable Germany I made true friends who aided me, and doing any honest work by day, I gave my nights to study, trying to repair the loss of years.

"Southern trees grow rapidly, for their sap is stirred by whirlwinds and fed with ardent heats. Fast I struggled up, groping for the light that dawned more fairly as I climbed; and when ten years were gone I seemed to have been born anew. Paul the slave was dead and his grave grown green; Paul the man had no part in him beyond the mournful memory of the youth that pined and died too soon. The world had done me a great wrong, yet I asked no atonement but the liberty to prove myself a man; no favor but the right to bury my dead past and make my future what I would. Other men's ambitions were not mine, for twenty years had been taken from me and I had no time to fight for any but the highest prize. I was grateful for the boon heaven sent me, and felt that my work was to build up an honest life, to till the nature given me, and sow therein a late harvest, that my sheaf might yet be worthy the Great Reaper's hand. If there be any power in sincere desire, any solace in devout belief,—that strength, that consolation will be mine. Man's opprobrium may oppress me, woman's pity may desert me, suffering and wrong may still pursue me,—yet I am not desolate; for when all human charities have cast me off I know that a Diviner love will take me in."

To Paul's voice came the music of a fervent faith, in his eye burned the fire of a quenchless hope, and on his countenance there shone a pale serenity that touched it with the youth time cannot take away. Past and present faded from his sight, for in that moment his spirit claimed its birthright, and beyond the creature of his love, his heart beheld the aspiration of his life.

"Claudia, I never thought to know affection like your own; never thought I could deserve so great a blessing; but when it came to me in tenderest guise, pleading to be taken in, how could I bar the door to such a welcome visitant? I did not, and the strong sweet angel entered in to kindle on my lonely hearth a household fire that can never die. Heaven help me if the ministering spirit goes!"

Through all the story of his own despairs and griefs Paul had not faltered, but gone resolutely on, painting his sufferings lightly for Claudia's sake, but now when he remembered the affection she had cherished, the anguish she might feel, the confidence she might believe betrayed, a keen remorse assailed him, and his courage failed. He thought of Claudia lost, and with an exclamation of passionate regret paced the long room with restless feet—paused for a little, looking out into the magic stillness of the night, and came back calm again.

"When you first gave me the good gift you have a right to take again, I told you I was orphaned, friendless, poor; but I did not tell you why I was thus desolate, believing it was wiser to leave a bitter history untold. I thought I did no wrong, but I have learned that perfect peace is only found in perfect truth; and I accept the lesson, for I was too proud of my success, and I am cast down into the dust to climb again with steadier feet. I let you judge me as an equal, showing you my weaknesses, my wants, my passions, and beliefs, as any happier lover might have done; you found some spark of manhood there, for you loved me, and that act should have made me worthier of the gift—but it did not. Claudia, forgive me; I was weak, but I struggled to be strong; for in the blissful months that have gone by, you showed me all your heart, enriched me with your confidence, and left no sorrow of your life untold—this brave sincerity became a mute reproach to me at last, for far down in *my* heart was a secret chamber never opened to your eye, for there my lost youth lay so stark and cold I dared not show you its dead face. But as the time came nearer when you were to endow me with the name which should go hand in hand with innocence and truth, this vague remorse for a silent wrong determined me to make confession of my past. I wrote it all, believing I could never tell it, as I have done to-night, learning that love can cast out fear. I wrote it and brought it many times, but never gave it, for O, Claudia! O, my heart! I loved you more than honor, and I could not give you up!"

From sleeping garden and still night a breath of air sighed through the room, as mournful and as sweet as those impassioned words, but Claudia never lifted up her hidden face, or stirred to answer it, for she was listening to a more divine appeal, and taking counsel in the silence of her heart.

Paul watched her, and the shadow of a great fear fell upon his face.

"I brought this confession here to-night, resolved to give it and be satisfied; but you did not come to meet me, and while I waited my love tempted me; the strong moment passed, and I burned it, yielding the nobler purpose for the dearer peace. This single page, how dropped I cannot tell, betrayed me to that— woman, and her malice forced on me the part I was not brave enough to play alone.

"Now, Claudia, all is told. Now, seeing what I have been, knowing what I desired to be, remembering mercifully what I am, try my crime and adjudge my punishment."

There was no need of that appeal, for judgment had been given long before the prayer came. Pride, and fear, and shame had dropped away, leaving the purer passion free; now justice and mercy took love by the hand and led it home. On Claudia's face there came a light more beautiful than any smile; on cheek and forehead glowed the fervor of her generous blood, in eye and voice spoke the courage of her steadfast heart, as she flung down the barrier, saying only: "Mine still, mine forever, Paul!" and with that tender welcome took the wronged man to the shelter of her love.

Tears hot and heavy as a summer rain baptised the new born peace and words of broken gratitude sang its lullaby, as that strong nature cradled it with blessings and with prayers. Paul was the weaker now, and Claudia learned the greatness of past fear by the vehemence of present joy, as they stood together tasting the sweetness of a moment that enriched their lives.

"Love, do you remember what this gift may cost? Do you remember what I am henceforth to other eyes? Can you bear to see familiar faces growing strange to you, to meet looks that wound you with their pity, to hear words that sting you with their truth, and find a shadow falling on your life from me?"

As he spoke, Paul lifted up that face, "clear-shining after rain," but it did not alter, did not lose its full content, as Claudia replied with fervent voice: "I do remember that I cannot pay too much for what is priceless; that when I was loveless and alone, there came a friend who never will desert me when all others fail; that from lowly places poets, philosophers, and kings have come; and when the world sneers at the name you give me, I can turn upon it saying with the pride that stirs me now: 'My husband has achieved a nobler success than men you honor, has surmounted greater obstacles, has conquered sterner foes, and risen to be an honest man.'"

Paul proved that he was one by still arming her against himself, still warning her of the cruel prejudices which he had such sad cause to know and fear.

"Your generous nature blinds you to the trials I foresee, the disappointments I foretell. In your world there will be no place for me, when this is known, and I cannot ask you to come down from your high place to sit beside an outcast's fire. I have not lost your love,—that was the blow I feared; and still possessing it I can relinquish much, and yield the new title I was soon to know, if I may keep the dear old one of 'friend.' It is no longer in our power to keep this secret unknown, and strengthen our affection by it, as I once hoped. Think of this, Claudia, in a calmer mood, weigh well the present and the future cost, for you have the power to make or mar your happiness.

"No loss of yours must be my gain, and I had rather never look into this face again than live to see it saddened by a vain regret for any act I might have saved you from by timely pain."

"I will consider, I will prove myself before I take your peace into my hands; but, Paul, I know the answer that will come to all my doubts, I know I shall not change."

Claudia spoke steadily, for she knew herself; and when at length her lover went, her last words were, "Believe in me, I shall not change."

Slowly the clear flame of the lamp grew dim and died, softly Night sang her cradle hymn to hush the weary world, and solemnly the silence deepened as the hours went by, but Claudia with wakeful eyes trod to and fro, or sat an image of mute thought. She was not alone, for good and evil spirits compassed her about, making that still room the battle-field of a viewless conflict between man's law, and woman's love. All the worldly wisdom time had taught, now warned her of the worldly losses she might yet sustain, all the prejudices born of her position and strengthened by her education now assailed her with covert skill, all the pride grown with her growth now tempted her to forget the lover in the slave, and fear threatened her with public opinion, that grim ghost that haunts the wisest and the best. But high above the voice of pride, the sigh of fear, and the echo of "the world's dread laugh," still rose the whisper of her heart, undaunted, undismayed, and cried to her,—

"I was cold, and he cherished me beside his fire; hungry, and he gave me food; a stranger, and he took me in."

Slowly the moon climbed the zenith and dropped into the West, slowly the stars paled one by one, and the gray sky kindled ruddily as dawn came smiling from the hills. Slowly the pale shadow of all worldliness passed from Claudia's mind, and left it ready for the sun, slowly the spectral doubts, regrets and fears vanished one by one, and through the twilight of that brief eclipse arose the morning of a fairer day.

As young knights watched their arms of old in chapels haunted by the memory of warrior or saint, and came forth eager for heroic deeds, so Claudia in the early dawn braced on the armor consecrated by a night of prayerful vigil, and with valiant soul addressed herself to the duty which would bring her life's defeat or victory.

Paul found another Claudia than the one he left; for a woman steadfast and strong turned to him a countenance as full of courage as of cheer, when standing there again he looked deep into her eyes and offered her his hand as he had done on that betrothal night. Now, as then, she took it, and in a moment gave a sweet significance to those characters which were the only vestiges of his wrong, for bending she touched the scarred palm with her lips, and whispered tenderly, "My love, there is no anguish in that brand, no humiliation in that claim, and I accept the bondage of the master who rules all the world."

As he spoke, Paul looked a happier, more *contented* slave, than those fabulous captives the South boasts of, but finds it hard to show.

Claudia led him back into the lower world again by asking with a sigh—"Paul, why should Jessie Snowden wish to wound me so? What cause have I given her for such dislike?"

A swift color swept across her lover's face, and the disdainful smile touched his lips again as he replied, "It is not a thing for me to tell; yet for the truth's sake I must. Jessie Snowden wooed what Claudia won. Heaven knows I have no cause for vanity, yet I could not help seeing in her eyes the regard it took so long to read in these more maidenly ones. I had no return to make, but gave all the friendship and respect I could to one for whom I had a most invincible distaste. There was no other cause for her dislike, yet I believe she hated me, or why should she speak with such malicious pleasure where a more generous woman would have held her peace? I have no faith in her, and by tomorrow I shall see in some changed face the first cloud of the storm she once foretold. Claudia, let us be married quietly, and go away until the gossips are grown weary, and we are forgotten."

Paul spoke with the sudden impulse of a nature sensitive and proud, but Claudia's energy was fully aroused and she answered with indignant color, "No, nothing must be changed. I asked my friends to see me made a proud and happy wife; shall I let them think I am ashamed to stand before them with the man I love? Paul, if I cannot bear a few harsh words, a few cold looks, a little pain, for you, of what worth is my love, of what use is my strength, and how shall I prove a fit friend and help-meet to you in the heavier cares and sorrows heaven sends us all?"

"Claudia, you are the braver of the two! I should be stronger if I had much to give; but I am so poor, this weight of obligation robs me of my courage. I am a weak soul, love, for I cannot trust, and I am still haunted by the fear that I shall one day read some sorrowful regret in this face, grown so wan with one night's watching for my sake."

Claudia dropped on her knee before him, and lifting up her earnest countenance, said, "Read it, Paul, and never doubt again. You spoke once of atonement,—make it by conquering your pride and receiving as freely as I give; for believe me, it is as hard a thing greatly to accept, as it is bountifully to bestow. You are not poor, for there can be no mine and thine between us two; you are not weak, for I lean on your strength, and know it will not fail; you are not fearful now, for looking here, you see the wife who never can regret or know the shadow of a change." Paul brushed the brown locks back, and as he read it smiled again, for heart and eyes and tender lips confirmed the truth, and he was satisfied.

Jessie Snowden's secret haunted her like Lady Macbeth's, and like that strong-minded woman, she would have told it in her sleep, if she had not eased herself by confiding it to a single friend. "Dear Maria" promised an eternal silence, but "Dear Maria" was the well known "little bird" who gave the whisper to the air. Rumor sowed it broadcast, gossips nurtured it, and Claudia reaped a speedy harvest of discomforts and chagrins.

She thought herself well armed for the "war of words"; but women's tongues forged weapons whose blows she could not parry, and men's censure or coarse pity pierced her shield, and wounded deeper than she dared to tell. Her "dear five hundred friends" each came to save her from social suicide, and her peaceful drawing-room soon became a chamber of the Inquisition, where a daily "Council of Ten" tormented her with warnings, entreaties—and reproaches,—harder trials for a woman to bear, than the old tortures of rack and thirst and fire.

She bore herself bravely through these troublous times, but her pillow received bitter tears, heard passionate prayers and the throbbing of an indignant heart, that only calmed itself by the power of its love. Paul never saw a tear or heard a sigh,—for him the steady smile sat on her lips, a cheerful courage filled her eye; but he read her pain in the meekness which now beautified her face, and silently the trial now drew them nearer than before.

There was no mother to gather Claudia to her breast with blessings and with prayers when the marriage morning dawned, no sister to hover near her, April-like, with smiles and tears, no father to give her proudly to the man she loved, and few friends to make it a blithe festival; but a happier bride had never waited for her bridegroom's coming than Claudia as she looked out at the sunshine of a gracious day, and said within herself, "Heaven smiles upon me with auspicious skies, and in the depths of my own heart I hear a sweeter chime than any wedding bells can ring,—feel a truer peace than human commendation can bestow. Oh father, whom I never knew! oh mother, whom I wholly loved! be with me now, and bless me in this happy hour."

Paul came at last, fevered with the disquiet of much sleepless thought, and still disturbed by the gratitude of a generous nature, which believed itself unworthy of the gift relenting

Fortune now bestowed. He saw a fair woman crowned for him, and remembering his past, looked at her, saying with troubled and agitated voice—"Claudia, it is not yet too late." But the white shape fluttered from him to the threshold of the door, and looking back, only answered, "Come."

Music, the benignant spirit of their lives, breathed a solemn welcome as the solitary pair paced down the chancel, through the silken stir of an uprising throng. Down from the altar window, full of sacred symbols and rich hues, fell heaven's benediction in a flood of light, touching Paul's bent head with mellow rays, and bathing Claudia's bridal snow in bloom.

Silently that unconscious pair preached a better sermon than had ever echoed there, for it appealed to principles that never die, and made its text, "The love of liberty, the liberty of love."

Many a worldly man forgot his worldliness, and thinking of Paul's hard-won success, owned that he honored him. Many a frivolous woman felt her eye wet by sudden dew, her bosom stirred by sudden sympathy, as Claudia's clear, "I will," rose through the hush, and many a softened heart confessed the beauty of the deed it had condemned.

Stern bridegroom and pale bride, those two had come into the chapel's gloom; proud-eyed husband, blooming wife, those two made one, passed out into the sunlight on the sward, and down along that shining path they walked serenely into their new life.

The nine days' wonder died away and Paul and Claudia, listening to the murmur of the sea, forgot there was a world through all that happy month. But when they came again and took their places in the circle they had left, the old charm had departed; for prejudice, a sterner autocrat than the Czar of all the Russias, hedged them round with an invisible restraint, that seemed to shut them out from the genial intercourse they had before enjoyed. Claudia would take no hand that was not given as freely to her husband, and there were not many to press her own as cordially as they once had done. Then she began to realize the emptiness of her old life, for now she looked upon it with a clearer eye, and saw it would not stand the test she had applied.

This was the lesson she had needed, it taught her the value of true friendship, showed her the poverty of old beliefs, the bitterness of old desires, and strengthened her proud nature by the sharp discipline of pain.

Paul saw the loneliness that sometimes came upon her when her former pleasures ceased to satisfy, and began to feel that his forebodings would prove true. But they never did; for there came to them those good Samaritans who minister to soul as well as sense; these took them by the hand, and through their honor for her husband, gave to Claudia the crowning lesson of her life.

They led her out of the world of wealth, and fashion, and pretense, into that other world that lies above it, full of the beauty of great deeds, high thoughts and humble souls, who walk its ways, rich in the virtues that

"Smell sweet, and blossom in the dust."

Like a child in fairyland she looked about her, feeling that here she might see again the aspirations of her youth, and find those happy visions true.

In this new world she found a finer rank than any she had left, for men whose righteous lives were their renown, whose virtues their estate, were peers of this realm, whose sovereign was Truth, whose ministers were Justice and Humanity, whose subjects all "who loved their neighbor better than themselves."

She found a truer chivalry than she had known before, for heroic deeds shone on her in the humblest guise, and she discovered knights of a nobler court than Arthur founded, or than Spenser sang. Saint Georges, valiant as of old, Sir Guyons, devout and strong, and silver-tongued Sir Launcelots without a stain, all fighting the good fight for love of God and universal right.

She found a fashion old as womanhood and beautiful as charity, whose votaries lived better poems than any pen could write; brave Britomarts redressing wrongs, meek Unas succoring the weak, high-hearted Maids of Orleans steadfast through long martyrdoms of labor for the poor, all going cheerfully along the by-ways of the world, and leaving them the greener for the touch of their unwearied feet.

She found a religion that welcomed all humanity to its broad church, and made its priest the peasant of Judea who preached the Sermon on the Mount.

Then, seeing these things, Claudia felt that she had found her place, and putting off her "purple of fine linen," gave herself to earnest work, which is the strengthening wine of life. Paul was no longer friendless and without a home, for here he found a country, and a welcome to that brotherhood which makes the whole world kin; and like the pilgrims in that fable never old, these two "went on their way rejoicing," leaving the shores of "Vanity Fair" behind them, and through the "Valley of Humiliation" climbed the mountains whence they saw the spires of the "Celestial City" shining in the sun.

Slowly all things right themselves when founded on truth. Time brought tardy honors to Paul, and Claudia's false friends beckoned her to come and take her place again, but she only touched the little heads, looked up into her husband's face, and answered with a smile of beautiful content—"I cannot give the substance for the shadow,—cannot leave my world for yours. Put off the old delusions that blind you to the light, and come up here to me."

ACKNOWLEDGMENTS

This twenty-first-century publication of William G. Allen's pamphlets and Louisa May Alcott's story "M.L." was inspired almost forty years ago in seminars with Professor David Brion Davis. He sent me, and many other students, "to the archives"; in Cornell University's Anti-Slavery Collection I read and hand-copied "The American Prejudice Against Color." John Weingartner encouraged the project, ensuring the narratives' publication in these times. Lori Vandermark brought my scribbles into the modern world of photocopy and computer.

Madeleine B. Stern and Leona Rostenberg offered their wisdom and scholarship as I linked the Alcott and May families from Boston to Syracuse, New York, and thence to Allen and Mary King's story. Professor R. J. M. Blackett rescued the "forgotten professor," restoring King and Allen to their rightful place in the Anglo-American abolitionist movement. Professor Milton Sernett kindly shared his research, mapping the "North Star country" for our band of brothers and sisters. Professor John Stauffer and Tavia N'ongo continue in the D.B.D tradition of comradely scholarship, as does Kevin Tanner.

My thanks to Professor Anna Davin and the members of *History Workshop Journal* who still keep faith with Anglo-American abolitionism. Professor Margaret Washington's kindness, integrity, and invaluable scholarship remind me that Sojourner Truth, William G. Allen, Mary King Allen, Samuel J. May, and Louisa May Alcott fought for the dignity and freedom of all creatures great and small.